BEHIND THE WAR IN ERITREA

BEHIND THE WAR
IN ERITREA

edited by
Basil Davidson, Lionel Cliffe and
Bereket Habte Selassie

SPOKESMAN

First published in 1980 by:
Spokesman
Bertrand Russell House
Gamble Street
Nottingham

Cloth ISBN 0 85124 301 0
Paper ISBN 0 85124 302 0

Printed by the Russell Press Ltd., Nottingham

CONTENTS

Preface

Lack of public attention is no measure of the importance of the Eritrean issue. The war of liberation from Ethiopian over-rule that has been going on there since 1961 is the longest war in Africa's history. It has already claimed perhaps 50,000 casualties, and over a million people have been displaced from their homes, the majority as refugees in the Sudan. The long-run fate of the 3½ million Eritreans depends on its outcome. Its significance to the area around and to broader strategic issues has always been heightened by the involvement of outside powers. But where once a 'feudal' Ethiopian empire got military backing from the United States, the fact of Soviet and Cuban involvement with a 'revolutionary' military regime in Ethiopia since 1977 points the need for a new assessment of the Eritrean question, but also of the Soviet role in Africa.

To the scale of fighting and the international implications must, however, be added another reason why the Eritrean liberation struggle must command attention: for what it tells us about the 'politics of liberation' in Africa today. As several of our contributions bear out, the Eritrean struggle does at its best exhibit some of the same characteristics as other guerilla wars of national liberation: the mobilisation of popular support, a commitment to self-reliance, and the coupling of elements of a social revolution to a national struggle. But there are differences. The context of the struggle — against a fellow African State as the 'colonial' power, rather than a western country, or a white minority regime — forces us to rethink the nature of 'imperialism' and also what the 'national question' means in Africa.

Yet any assessment of the Eritrean Liberation struggle and the profound issues it raises is made the more difficult because of the paucity of reliable information, not only from its fluctuating course at any one moment but about its origins and character. With these needs in mind, an International Symposium was held in London in January 1979. The sessions, which were chaired by Basil Davidson, were each organised around a presentation by one member of a panel of experts who had studied some aspect of the Eritrean story. The symposium was the first of its kind in Britain, and perhaps anywhere, in bringing together historians and other analysts, activists and several outside observers who had seen events at first hand. Their reports

sparked off, and were in turn fleshed out by, lively discussion among
an audience of a couple of hundred that included Eritreans, Ethiopians
and other Africans, as well as many concerned participants from
Europe and North America as well as Britain.

The presentations, as they have been revised in the light of these
discussions, form the body of this book. None of them would claim to
provide a definitive evaluation of the Eritrean liberation struggle, nor
do they together provide an exhaustive survey of all its dimensions.
However, they do represent a compilation of the information that was
available, though not widely, at a certain point in time. They also cover
a range of the most crucial questions: they do touch on all the major
historical stages; they discuss the social and economic content as well as
the political and military experiences of the struggle. Their publication
thus seemed to be warranted, even if it is not the last word or if recent
events have rendered some of the material dated.

It should also be emphasised that each contributor was free to
present his own assessments and conclusions, and no attempt has been
made in the editing to reconcile the detailed points of disagreement or
differences in interpretation. Yet the differing materials still illustrate
an impressive degree of consensus on the broad issues: the right of the
Eritrean people to nationality and self-determination; the social revolution initiated by the Eritrean People's Liberation Front; condemnation
of Soviet support for Ethiopian offensives.

This volume would not have been possible without the efforts of
Bereket Habte Selassie who initiated the symposium, of War on Want
who gave it their backing, and of Mary Dines who organised it and
whose help in the preparation for publication has been invaluable.

Basil Davidson, Lionel Cliffe and Bereket Habte Selassie
October, 1979

PART I
ERITREA'S HISTORICAL CLAIMS TO NATIONHOOD

An Historical Note
Basil Davidson

The following brief notes on Eritrean history are intended as a background to a consideration, within an African revolutionary perspective, of the liberation struggle in Eritrea of today. As with all such processes, this struggle cannot be understood outside its own historical framework.

The origins and self-identification of the people of this country lie far back in time. This people emerges in modern history, during the 19th century, as a group of independent chiefdoms and clans. They had trading relations with other Red Sea peoples along the seaboard, and with their Tigrayan and Amharic neighbours to their westward in the hills beyond the Mareb valley. But they were subject to none of these neighbours.

The definition of their country as Eritrea, with its frontiers, derived from the imperial partnership and rivalry of two expansionist powers late in the 19th century, Ethiopia and Italy.

Italian colonial enterprises got off to a slow start, deriving partly from Italy's economic backwardness, political newness as a single united country, and the domination of the scene by Britain and France. There was much opposition to colonial adventures, and only a hesitant support for them by the banking and industrial bourgeoisie of the northern cities.

So far as the Horn of Africa is concerned (and I am here omitting Somalia), Italy's 'presence' dates from the purchase by a Genoese ship-owner, in 1869, of a strip of seaboard in the Bay of Assab, far to the south on the western side of the Red Sea. Nothing much came of this purchase, and the story of Italian colonisation of the region really begins in 1885, when an Italian force occupied the little port of Massawa. They were able to do this with British diplomatic backing, the British government of the day finding it convenient to have a junior partner in the 'colonial share-out', here in the north-east, just as the British also found it convenient to have another such junior partner, Portugal, in the western regions of Africa.

From Massawa the Italians pushed inland on military conquest. They did not find this easy, being stiffly defeated (at Dogali) by Eritrean fighters in 1887 and continuing to face Eritrean armed resistance. Gradually, however, they continued inland; and this is where the other imperialist element entered on the scene, that of Amharic Ethiopia.

Italian pressure coincided with the rise to power of the builder of the modern Ethiopian empire, Menelik, at that time *negus* or king of the Amharic province of Shoa but in rivalry for the imperial throne with the then Emperor John.

The Italian government (that of Crispi) wished to establish a coastal colony and, secondly, to extend Italian 'protection' over the whole of what was known as Abyssinia. Pursuing these aims, Crispi believed that helping Menelik to become emperor would open the door to Italy's imperialist penetration. Menelik, for his part, appears to have understood Crispi's game perfectly well, and to have received Italian aid (notably in arms) with his eyes open. In March 1889 the Emperor John fell in battle while attempting to push Ethiopian (that is, Amharic) imperial influence beyond Tigray. Menelik at once proclaimed himself emperor (though without the agreement of a number of Ethiopian notabilities, including Ras Mangascia of Tigray, John's son); and the Italians were able to secure from him a treaty of friendship and alliance (Uccialli, May 1889). Following this, the Italian invaders rapidly took Keren (June) and Asmara (August) against continued Eritrean resistance, and on 1 January 1890 proclaimed the territory which they had now more or less occupied as their colony of Eritrea.

This alarmed Menelik, who now saw that the trap of Italian 'partnership' might well be sprung on him unless he reacted with energy. In 1893 he accordingly denounced the Treaty of Uccialli, holding that the Italian version which gave Italy a 'protectorate' over Ethiopia was null and void, since it did not appear in the Amharic version and he, Menelik, had not agreed to it. Greatly underestimating Menelik's military and political strength, the Italians proceeded to challenge him on his own ground. This led to their great military disaster at Adua in 1896, when more Italians were killed in one day than in all the battles for the unification of Italy itself.

The defeat at Adua put paid to Italian aspirations for a protectorate over Ethiopia, but it also led to their consolidation of their colony of Eritrea. Menelik renounced his own ambitions in that country, and signed peace with Italy a few months after the battle of Adua (that is, in October 1896).

The Italian colony of Eritrea lasted from 1890 until 1941. Gradually, Eritrean resistance to Italian rule came to an end, and, as with other colonies formed in the same period, the peoples living within it were subjected to a contradictory experience. On the one hand, they were robbed of their independence and made subject to a foreign rule and culture which denied their own culture and identity. On the other hand, the fact of living together within frontiers which were now defined as those of a separate entity, Eritrea, gave them a new sense of common fate and of incipient nationhood.

A few more dates may be useful here. Using Eritrea as their base, the armies of Fascist Italy invaded Ethiopia in 1935, crossing the Mareb on 3 October. Ethiopian resistance was prolonged, but failed in the end for want of any foreign aid. Fascist Italy proclaimed its possession of the Ethiopian empire on 5 May 1936. Then came the second world war. Mussolini delayed entering it until he felt sure that he knew who was going to win. With the fall of France in June 1940, this seemed to be Nazi Germany. Italy accordingly declared war on Britain and France on 10 June 1940. Having very strong forces in East Africa, initially totalling some 300,000 under arms, Fascist Italy at first put Britain on the defensive in the Horn of Africa. But the tide was soon reversed, and by 1941 British armies had swept Italian rule from the scene. Ethiopia was returned to the Emperor (Haile Selassie), and Eritrea was placed under a British provisional administration. Ultimate responsibility for what should happen there now lay with the newly-created United Nations Organisation.

What was now the population of Eritrea? The following approximate numbers relate to the period before 1945, and may be taken as very roughly accurate, at least as a guide. The total population was given as being 758,000, although this, like most colonial population estimates, was probably smaller than the truth. Of this total, 565,000 were counted as sedentary, and 193,000 as nomadic. They belonged to a number of religions of which the most important were Coptic (given as 371,000) and Muslim (given as 341,000). They spoke a number of languages of which the most important were Tigrinya (given as 371,000) and Tigray (fairly close to Tigrinya, and given as 175,000). Other languages, spoken by smaller and sometimes very small groups, included Beja, Bilein, Saho, Afar, Arabic (given as 37,000) and Nilotic.

And it is in this period, towards the end of outright colonial rule and in the period of British provisional government, that the constellation of nationalities which had long formed the Eritrean population began — as elsewhere in Africa — to come to terms with the concept of a common nationhood, and therefore of a common nationalism.

In occupying Eritrea, Britain made it clear that she would not stay, and promised the Eritreans that they should never return to Italian rule. What then should become of Eritrea? The foreign ministers of the four Great Powers found it difficult to agree on the answer, while a joint commission of investigation sent to find it on the spot also failed to reach agreement. These were early days in the rise of modern African nationalism, and imperialist decolonisation was not yet on the agenda. It was still a time when Europe decided for Africa. What should they decide was 'best for the Eritreans'?

An insight into imperialist thought on the subject may be had from the British chief administrator of Eritrea during 1942-44. Writing in 1945, S.H. Longrigg (*A Short History of Eritrea*, Oxford, 1945, page 171) opined that an independent state of Eritrea 'could not but end in anarchy, or in renewed European control', because 'there exists no imaginable governing or administrative class'. It was a familiar kind of judgement for those days; but even when leaving it aside, the evidence suggests that the idea of Eritrean nationhood was still relatively weak among such Eritrean notabilities as may have been consulted.

In this situation the United Nations decided in 1950 that Eritrea should become a federated state within the Ethiopian empire, and this federation duly came into existence on 11 September 1952, when an Eritrean assembly chose as chief executive a man called Tedla Bairu, who at that time was leader of the party favouring union with Ethiopia. Note however that this was federation, not complete absorption. The Ethiopian emperor and government had desired complete absorption, but they did not get it. One may here recall another judgement of that same British administrator in his book of 1945. 'Against the sometimes advocated assignment of the whole (of Eritrea) to Ethiopia (which would accept and indeed actively claims it)', he wrote, 'is the certainty that much of Eritrea was never Ethiopian; that such parts could not be suitably or acceptably ruled by that government; and that *no part has been politically Ethiopian* since the deliberate cession of Beyond-the-Mareb by Menelik (i.e. in 1889)' (*loc.cit.*, my emphasis).

Baulked in 1952, the Ethiopian imperialists bided their time. Meanwhile they saw to it that the Eritrean assembly should sufficiently reflect the views which they meant to prevail. And on 14 November 1962, ten years later, they were able to induce that Assembly to vote for an end to the federation, and for Eritrea's incorporation as an integral part of the Ethiopian empire. This decision was immediately contested by other Eritreans; and a war of independence was launched almost at once.

Onwards from 1962 the Ethiopian regime governed, or attempted to govern, Eritrea on straightforward colonial lines: that is, with the introduction of Amharic authority at all decisive points; with the suppression in education and public life of Tigrinya and other local languages in favour of the Amharic language; with the exclusion of any specific Eritrean identity, right to decision, or control over local development; and, increasingly, with the use of military force to suppress all signs or claims of Eritrean independence. They applied to Eritrea, in other words, exactly the same colonialist policies and practices which they had long applied to the Somalis of the Ogaden.

The case against Ethiopian possession of Eritrea was and is, therefore, qualitatively no different from the case against any other colonial enclosure. If it was right for the European colonial powers to be thrust from their possessions overseas, then it is similarly right for the Ethiopians to be denied possession of Eritrea (and, no less, of the Ogaden, enclosed within the Ethiopian empire at almost the same time as Eritrea became an Italian colony).

What should now become the destiny of Eritrea is the subject of this symposium, and it is for the Eritreans themselves to answer. An observer can note three central points:

a. If a sense of Eritrean nationhood, of Eritrean nationalism, was evidently weak in the European colonial period (as it was weak in many parts of Africa), it is evidently no longer so today. With the growth of a movement of and struggle for national liberation, and above all after the crystallisation within that struggle of the Eritrean People's Liberation Front (EPLF), the people of Eritrea have begun to make their own history again. They reach back to the themes of independence and identity that were stifled by Italian rule after 1890. They react to the challenge of the outside world of today as other African peoples have reacted: that is, they seek the establishment of identity and independence within a national framework. This is the modern and modernising development of their own history.

b. To the very obvious limits and frustrations of nationalism within the neo-colonial model (and I assume there is no need here to define what is meant by neo-colonial model), the Eritreans through the EPLF reply with a revolutionary perspective. To the alternatives suggested by Longrigg in 1945 — anarchy or resumed foreign rule (whether direct or indirect) — they add another. This third alternative, now in process, is the building of social, cultural, political and economic structures 'from the base', through which, by the processes of evoking and promoting mass participation in self-rule, the people of Eritrea (as distinct from Eritrean notabilities) take power within their own hands and govern themselves. This too is the modern and modernising development of their own history.

c. In acting thus, the Eritreans have placed themselves in midstream of Africa's revolutionary trend and perspective. With other liberation movements engaged in the same kinds of process, they shut the door on neo-colonialism as well as on colonialism. They give themselves the chance and scope to solve the problems of their own heritage, whether pre-colonial, or neo-colonial. Beyond that, they also put themselves on the road to solve, in the measure that their neighbours take the same road, the problems of their national destiny within the whole region of the Horn.

It follows that the Eritrean liberation movement, as crystallised in its most developed form, deserves the close attention and the active support of all those persons, parties and movements elsewhere who believe that the interests of their own countries, and the interests of African progress, are the same.

Pre-Colonial and Colonial History
Richard Greenfield

No people have unique claims to history. Every peoples and every nation in Africa – as elsewhere – has three thousand years of history – and more – behind it. My subject, specifically the history of Eritrea, is therefore important as a background to the understanding of the Eritrean revolution and, as Basil Davidson has pointed out, the significant role of Eritrea in the African revolution, which has to date received too little attention – although this is changing. I shall suggest to you that this understanding is particularly necessary in looking at the more recent history of Eritrea, for history is not only the accurate presentation and interpretation of the past: its comprehension is a continuous process. Relevant history, especially in times of struggle and revolution, is continuously being made. Indeed future historians may well interpret the 1970s as the most momentous period in the whole Eritrean experience. I have, however, been asked to concentrate on earlier times.

That said, it must be admitted that the topic given to me is still too vast for one short presentation. That fact, and my suspicion that many who later read this lecture will not be newcomers to the history of the horn of Africa, must justify a selective as well as an interpretive approach.

In the first place, the title "Pre-Colonial and Colonial" history begs a question. It implies, quite falsely, that colonialism is something Europe has done to Africa comparatively recently. But the experience of Eritrea is surely a much longer experience of colonialism. Examination of this contention raises the questions what were and are the policies in North-eastern Africa and what has been their relationship one with another? We have to re-examine the data, for these issues have to date been largely avoided by international scholarship. Why has this been so?

Escape from Traditional Historiography

With the passing of Ethiopia's emperors and the decay of empire we are losing another less obvious but connected phenomenon – the emperor's chroniclers. In the middle ages, priests fulfilled this function. More recently it must be admitted it has been foreign propagandists and even scholars who have served the imperial purpose. The result has not only been that the History of the Horn of Africa has tended to be portrayed as a history of one set of kings and their courtiers and bishops, rather than of whole peoples, but also that centres of nationalism other than at the then current imperial centre of the Abyssinian empire have been neglected. The cost of this less than objective approach is surely at last clear to everyone with the least familiarity with the contemporary history of North-eastern Africa. The imminence of the Ethiopian revolution was for this reason demonstrated scholastically by very few. Meantime the ship of state — an empire-state — sailed directly, rather than drifted, right onto the rocks. Predictably the reality was stoutly denied by the chorniclers — and by one at least even after the event.[1] Their view of Eritrea was similarly prejudiced.

Scholarship, in Europe particularly, is taking time to re-adjust. The writings of those who could not see their way to subscribe to such doctrines as the divine right of kings (with non-African origins) were omitted from bibliographies and even castigated in that absence. But had they really understood the traditions of Abyssinia, they should not have been surprised. There is clear parallel in how easy it was for a king, having placed his bottom on a throne, to ignore and replace a genealogist who failed to grasp the role expected of him. Who then has been left to describe events? Although a modern history of the whole region has yet to be attempted, tomorrow's historians will undoubtedly find themselves indebted to the so-called ephemeral writings of Eritreans and others and to the work of a number of serious foreign journalists — several of whom have demonstrated a high degree of scholarly detachment and perception. And even if no sycophant at court can be a reliable guide to regional politics, remember that a critical re-reading can on occasion prove revealing both in what is included and perhaps misinterpreted and what is denied. A great task lies before us all; to re-examine and reassess all the sources.

Also relevant has been a wider lack of precision in the use of terminology — inherited from colonial studies. Take the terms 'nation' and 'tribe'. Vast social organisations, such as those of the Zulu, Oromo and Ibo millions have for instance been termed 'tribes', whilst 75,000 Luxembourgers have qualified as a 'nation'. Failure to recognise the Kikuyu and the Zulu as nations had led not infrequently to the theory, or more properly the assumption, that all 'nationalism' in Africa and therefore 'nations' in Africa, have grown completely out of recent colonial experience. Such an argument is basically ethnic — its attraction to such otherwise distinguished historians as Hugh Trevor Roper notwithstanding.

Imperialism in Antiquity

Wherever there were people there was politics, for man, as Aristotle taught, is a political animal. Wherever millions of people have been mobilised to pursue some common policy and to recognise some focus of authority within their corporate body politic – then nationalism and state-frameworks have developed. The European colonial period has been but a short and recent, if profoundly significant, period in the long history of the African people. Many nationalisms in the Horn of Africa, however, are very old as is their relationship one to another. On the other hand, in most general ways the frequently acclaimed 'uniqueness' of the Abyssinian-African experience is quite recent. Basil Davidson has already usefully distinguished between African nationalism and nationality. In this context let us look at the term 'imperialism'. Europe's were not the first – or the last – empires. Throughout Africa's history, where sufficient numbers of peoples have come to recognise some focus for their loyalty (and at least in the military sense, feel some responsibility in return) then this 'nationalism' has resisted others, seeking to impose power and authority without being able to evoke loyalty in response. This is imperialism. Such situations, and particularly feelings, of identity and loyalty can change. But it is suggested that such changing relationships between nationalisms and state-frameworks are the pattern of history – in Africa not least. And Africa has known its own 'homegrown' imperialisms, in differing times and regions.

Cultural developments amongst the peoples of North-eastern Africa, who were of course African, were nevertheless at periods much affected by a cultural overlay derived from migrations westward across the Red Sea throughout the several millenia preceding the Christian era. The converse was also true – indeed, modern scholarship is moving towards a questioning of the whole 'Semitic conspiracy' which to date has tended to attribute every innovation in language and living pattern to influence from the Middle East. Some cultural interchange occurred in every direction. Suffice it to conclude, therefore, that indigenous and developing techniques and patterns, both agricultural, commercial and political, largely inspired the establishment of city states, such as Yeha, Matara, etc., and (probably later, although work on recently revealed tombs is awaited) Aksum. Eritrean culture and civilisation is homegrown.

The wealth of these states was based on trade and taxation. In this context, a first century trader's account refers to one ruler, Zoscales, as 'mean and miserly in his ways and always grasping for more'. This ruler, whom most historians have conveniently equated with the Aksumite rulers and even with one particular ruler, Za Hakale – although there is insufficient evidence for either of these identifications and he could easily have been a coastal ruler – clearly enforced an economic function, the collection of taxes, which his subjects – if not visiting traders from overseas, from Sudan to the west and Abyssinia to the south – may have condoned and even appreciated.

We know little of the relationship between such rulers and the ruled – the word Eritrea is not new, so I will call them Eritreans. If they were nationals, we may still never know what proportion, if any, of the fiscal or material benefits derived by particular rulers were actually passed to vassals – or whether their acquiescence to authority was in return merely for the peace and order which the ruler's power ensured and which was necessary for the safety of their families and for their economic well-being. Nevertheless a relationship involving regulation, obedience and some degree of loyalty can be safely assumed. It is, after all, only in revolution that the nature of such relationships may be fundamentally altered. However if they were *not* nationals, then the relationship is clearer.

It is known of the city-state of Aksum, that the organisation which its ruler set up came to *dominate* other cities and a considerable area of north-eastern Africa – a fact perhaps not determined by, but far from unrelated to, the very considerable extent of trade in the area at the beginning of the first Christian millenium. Evidence for the reconstruction of this commercial activity can be drawn from the inscriptions of ancient Egypt and Persia, from numismatics and from other archaeological discoveries in Arabia as well as Eritrea, Ethiopia and the Nile Valley.

Almost certainly with the intention of securing greater control over this trade the ruler and people of the city of Aksum extended their influence to create an empire-state. The ruler adopted the title *Negusa-Neghest* or King of the Kings – perhaps originating in Persia as has been frequently suggested but nonetheless having a clear derivation: 'the exacting of tribute'. From inscriptions recorded at the port of Adulis on the Eritrean coast we know that one Aksumite ruler of pre-Christian times (the conversion was mid-fourth century) conducted conquests 'to make the people live in peace' into the mountains (?Simien) and the 'waterless plains of the frankincense country' (?Somalia), giving peoples 'instructions to guard the coast' of Eritrea and *restoring* their lands 'subject to the payment of tribute'. He also sent a fleet across the sea (to Arabia) and 'having reduced the sovereigns . . . imposed a land tribute' and charged them 'to make travelling safe by sea and by land'. He reduced 'the nations bordering' on his country as far as 'Sasu' (?Meroe). Political and para-military organisation made this possible. He comments, as might later chroniclers, 'some expeditions were conducted by myself in person and ended in victory (!) and the others I entrusted to my officers'. It was a story of conquest, 'pacification' and economic reorientation: in fact typical colonialism.

What was created was acknowledged to the greater credit and power of the king of the kings and his nationals, by other rulers of the world – such as the Emperor Constantine who compared Aksumites to Romans; another imperial race. It was clearly in their interest to retain their imposed sway as long as they could. History suggests that to hold an empire *by force* is possible, but expensive. A better method is to *integrate* the new components, to invoke a loyalty to the centre of the wider empire-state, i.e. to create and foster a new identity, a wider nationalism, to coincide with an expanded horizon – that of the empire-state. Most empires in history have attempted this one way or another. The question we must ask is, did the Eritreans and others integrate into the empire-state: it is not an issue of boundaries but of identity, for the empire-state of earlier periods in Aksum and elsewhere knew no exact linear boundaries only tributaries. In many, in fact nearly all, cases linear boundaries were a result of the 'expansion of Europe'. In Amharic 'tributary' not 'frontier' is the meaning of the word which much later Menelik II was to use in his correspondence with European rulers in the late nineteenth century. The limits of Aksumite power were merely the limits of the effective collection of tribute and slaves.

In the fourth century AD King of Kings Ezana (325-75 AD) demonstrated this concept of the tributary limits of an empire-state. He introduced himself in another inscription, as 'Ezana, the son of Ella Amida of the tribe of Halen, the King of Aksum and Himyar and of Raidan and Saba and of Salhen and of Siyamo and of Bega and of Kasu . . .' and explained how subjects of the empire-state, clearly not Aksumites but Noba of the vicinity of Meroe on the Nile, considered that they were beyond his reach in terms of tribute. They apparently estimated his limit as the Takkazze River, still so called. He caused to be written:

> I took the field against the Noba when the people of the Noba revolted,whentheyboasted and "he will not cross over the Takkazze" said the people of the Noba when they did violence to the people of Mangurto and Hasa and Barya and the Blacks and waged war on the Red people and a second and third time broke their oath and without consideration slew their neighbours and plundered our envoys and messengers whom I had sent to interrogate them, robbing them of their possessions and seizing their lances. When I sent again and they did not hear me and reviled me and made off, I took the field against them and I armed myself with the power of the Lord of the Land and fought on the Takkazze at the ford of Kemalke. Thereupon they took flight.

Ezana then went on to record the destruction he wrought,the names of fallen chieftains, the booty which he appropriated and incidentally the destruction or sacking of Meroe. The tributary limits of the Aksumite empire-state were clearly fluid: this indicates that as today, the colonized people did not accept that status willingly and Eritreans were among those people.

Nations in Medieval Times

The Eritrean people lived on the periphery of Abyssinia only occasionally affected by the authority of that empire-state. The medieval history of the latter can be represented as a series of cyclic expansions and withdrawals from one or other of a series of foci in northeastern Africa.

As Ethiopian history has normally been portrayed, withdrawals to the 'highland core of ancient Abyssinia' have been seen as general reverses for 'Ethiopian nationalism' — this is superficial. The corollary has been ignored that other nationalisms, which it has not been fashionable to study, may be shown to have thrived at such times. A further point suggests itself: that the Ethiopian empire was not (and is not yet) either a nation or a nation-state.

True nationalist sentiment draws strength from historical experience. Admittedly this is sometimes distorted, usually by exaggeration, by politicians for the purpose of nation-building. But one sure test is when historical experience is discontinued at a certain point through the breakdown of a state and nationalism nevertheless continues to exist as an aspiration. If the majority then adhere to it, then nationalism — indeed the nation — can be said to have survived. The Zulu and Ibo nations survive today without recognized state-frameworks. Thus we have also to ask, are the Eritreans, who are admittedly more culturally diverse, a nation, whether or not they were independent and united at every given time in the past. Was there a true national spirit? And does it live on?

In many respects the historically repetitive process above described, the insistent but cyclic expansionism of Abyssinia, resembles the history of China, the boundaries of whose effective rule have to this day varied greatly depending upon the authority or weakness of the central dynasty or government. To develop the analogy further, despite the current western reliance on treaties guaranteeing frontier lines, many Chinese are inclined to conceive of China as 'where the Chinese live' while recognizing that the degree of independence enjoyed by Mongolia, Manchuria, Korea, Tibet, etc., is dependent at any one time in history on the strength of inner China — the nucleus of that empire-state. The Chinese empire has enjoyed many millenia in which to develop and inspire 'wider nationalism' but whether or not the persons on her periphery *are* Chinese, is a matter *for their own decision*, affected, as such decisions must be, by those factors of which all nationalisms take account — linguistic or cultural features which improve communication; religious or ideological affinities, etc.

The *relevance* of this comparison — and it has been argued that the study of history should take account of relevance — is that it is what the concept of self-determination and the international agreements in which it is codified, are all about. If subjects of an empire persist in refusal to submerge and identify with a nearby imperialist group, are they not to be allowed freely to go their own way? Have the Eritreans or the Somalis — or the Irish for that matter — all decided to be citizens of a nearby empire-state? The issue is one of how they identify *themselves* — not each other. If they are resistant to identification and absorption, then their national history should be disentangled and restated. This is our task.

By the middle of the seventh century AD the Aksumite empire-state was collapsing. It was incapable either of expansion or even of maintaining stability since economic power, the basis of enforced obedience and unity, was also wilting. Hence the empire-state could not sustain itself. In due course, Aksum in the pattern of all empires, fell into decline and disintegrated. There was a number of political as well as economic reasons for this — including the resistance and growing power of the Beja — but they cannot be dealt with here. Meantime, the Eritrean-Afars formed part of the Adal kingdom and, later, the Sultanate of Aussa. In due course too, another significant Abyssinian state developed from centres of power located further south in the mountains of present day Ethiopia. The Abyssinian tradition recorded in later documents has it that Lasta, deep in the mountain fortresses of what is today the north of Ethiopia, became the new overall focus of power. Unfortunately, as has been argued, Ethiopian history has too long been represented merely as a catalogue of kings, and that interpretation of the story of the Zagwa rulers fits into such a chronological framework almost too readily. *The truth is that we know very little about Lasta and the Zagwa.* Roha, or Lalibela as it is more frequently called after one of the kings, was the capital and in the late sixties archaeologists discovered it to have been a walled city — walled against whom? We have little or no idea of the extent of the rulers' authority beyond those walls and hence do not know how many other foci and national loyalties existed in north-eastern Africa one thousand years ago. Nevertheless the Arab historians have much more to tell us, in the context of the history of the Eritrean region, than is widely known. They must be reread.

There is no evidence that either Lasta, or the more southerly Abyssinian dynasty that is described from the thirteenth century onwards as 'Solomonid', was paid regular tribute by any group of Eritreans. The Beja principalities for example were quite independent. Nor is the exaction of tribute in any case evidence of nationality as we have defined it: tribute was a form of insurance not infrequently paid in more than one direction. Also, it was often related to religious affinities unconnected with nationality. Nearer to today, we do know that in the sixteenth century the *Bahari Negash* or rulers of the sea held sway over parts of the coast and what came to be termed the *Medri Bahri*, an area perhaps roughly synonymous with the plateau regions of the Eritrea of today, more often than not as completely independent rulers. Abyssinian rulers repeatedly struggled to gain control of trade routes and ports. Since they met with little success they must have been resisted. Its geo-political position, however, eventually also exposed Eritrea to additional colonialisms — this time from the sea. Despite resistance, the Ummayad Caliphates occupied the prosperous trading centres that had developed on the Dahlak island archipelago and parts of the coast. The Barka lowlands and northern highlands paid tribute to the Fung rulers and later the Egyptians. Infrequent incursions from traditional directions by the Tigrai and Amhara rulers continued to be resisted, sometimes with the help of foreigners.

Again the way this has subsequently been recorded is a typical example of the Ethiopian chroniclers' technique against which we must be on our guard. When 'the empire had no firm focus (and) local chieftains became increasingly independent . . .' writes Ullendorff, 'material progress (and even) intellectual development was virtually unknown. There were occasional flutters of light, some able rulers, but the ensuing darkness (sic) was only the greater . . .' Although he is discussing the seventeenth and eighteenth centuries he finds it pertinent to add 'only in her rediscovered unity under the Emperors John, Menelik and Haile Sellasie does the country find its soul and genius again, its spirit and its sense of mission'.* But the frontiers of the Ethiopian empire-state were not 'rediscovered' nor was there anything but a facade of unity. And the mission of these monarchs was, at least to some extent, imperialist. Frontiers were negotiated with other participants in the scramble for Africa and they were reached in the same way as was the throne, according to ancient proverb, by 'wading in blood'.

Eritrea and the Scramble

The opening of the Suez Canal in 1869 greatly enhanced the strategic significance of the coastlines of the Red Sea and Gulf of Aden. A colonial struggle developed between the expansionist powers – Italy, Britain (and Egypt), France, Russia – and Shewa, for that peripheral southern province of Abyssinia in particular was moving to dominate the imperial quest of the Abyssinian chieftains and *rases*. However, in the north it was Italian colonial rule, established in the late nineteenth century, which finally unified the *Medri Bahri:* the Barka lowlands and the northern highlands; Massawa and the surrounding coastal plain and the Danakil lowlands – although the process may be said to have been begun by the Egyptians. These areas constitute present day Eritrea.

The attention of many scholars has been directed to the political history of European colonisation there, which throughout north-eastern Africa followed the traditional patterns: one sided 'protectorate' agreements; commercial houses giving way to imperial governments; excuses for 'punitive expeditions' and 'pacification' etc. Perhaps the only significant difference to be noted is that on the whole the colonial expeditions organized by representatives of European powers sought to discourage the slave trade while those of the Abyssinian rulers were not so orientated – quite the contrary.

However, the tone of future research must not stop at the impact of each of these aspects of imperialism on the people of Eritrea, it must

* E. Ullendorff, *The Ethiopians,* 3rd Edition (London, 1973), p.75.

seek to present their continuous and coherent development. The history of Africa is not the history of its invaders. Therefore the traditional sources bequeathed to us by the latter, although vitally important must needs be re-examined and used with caution. What was incidental to the colonial historian may well be vital to the Africanist — but it is equally probable that much of importance was not recorded there at all. A priority is therefore that indigenous oral and written material and what has been termed 'ephemera' must be collected and collated, as was begun in Ghana at the Institute of African Studies which Kwame Nkrumah officially opened in 1963 (although it had begun to function earlier).

Even obvious sources such as imperial Ethiopian letters and agreements have not all been analysed with a view to revealing the realities of Eritrea. More important however has been the economic factor. While governors and administrators came and went a vital and continuous process was occurring. I refer to the development of an indigenous working class — a class whose wider aspirations were Eritrean and among whom modern Eritrean nationalism as we know it today, was born. This indeed was the gestation period for all modern African nationalism, for Eritrea, like Ghana, Tanzania, Senegal, is a child of the African Revolution.

The Periods of Colonisation

Much work remains to be done on the Italian colonial period, but in summary, as I wrote in the early 1960's, under the Italians the ports of Eritrea had been merely dhow harbours, and communications with the plateau had been confined to the somewhat inefficient railway system, right until it was decided to invade Ethiopia. Then preparations led to the construction of spectacular roads and the growth of towns, but the criterion was always strategic, not economic. The Italian East African empire collapsed during World War II. British Officials were faced with the ruins of the Italian orientated colonial economy, the loss of individual savings, the inability and in any case unwillingness of the British to subsidise the territory, the consequent calamitous rise in taxation and in the cost of living etc. All caused severe economic distress to the whole population. But more than this there were returning soldiers from Libya and elsewhere, although not studied, every bit as politically conscious as their more celebrated brothers who, given neither jobs nor allowances, were to march in disillusion on the castle residence of the Governor-general in Accra, Ghana, on 28 February 1948.

The Eritrean economy soon reverted to pre-fascist — but not pre-Italian — levels. There was some competition for employment and inevitably, therefore, friction between the small Eritrean and the Italian working classes; there was resentment against the continued alienation of land, against arrogance of the Sudanese military and other employees of the British, and a growing suspicion of the goodwill of the latter. The atmosphere of repression induced by the former fascist government was to some extent alleviated, and this together with modest increases in educational opportunity led to the dissatisfaction and disaffection of both town and country areas coming to express itself more and more in political awareness and activity. Eritrean nationalism thrived.

It is within the overall setting of the African revolution that Italian colonialism in general and land policies in particular, and British military administration, *both* provided the culture in which modern Eritrean nationalism could develop. The Eritreans recognised a common historial experience. The catalyst was their growing and dissatisfied indigenous working class — ever more politically aware and stimulating a politically progressive Eritrean nationalism.

Much has been made of the 'promises' to the nationalists said to have been made in British leaflets dropped during World War II. There are however curious differences in presentation: some writers claim they offered 'self-determination'; others 'union with mother Ethiopia'. It is time we collected and published in full as many of these leaflets as can be recovered and examined the whole background to that propaganda exercise. Who wrote them for example, and with what in view? Without such study they are of little historical (as distinct from propaganda) value.

The British period saw one of the first political movements — the *Mahiber Fekri Hager* ('The party with love of the country' — or, the Patriotic Party) — emerge in 1942 and it soon had pamphlets and propaganda in circulation. A Unionist Party which worked closely with the Ethiopian Christian Church in Eritrea was also established. The Church under the leadership of Abune Markos was actively committed to a struggle for union with Ethiopia. British reports suggested that this was because the Ethiopian government was thought far more likely than the British to return the estates of which the Church had been dispossessed by the Italians, who had leased them to settlers and some of the poverty-stricken villagers. True the Christian Church was a great landowner in Tigrai to the south but, far more important, the Ethiopian Christian Church was at that time basic to the political philosophy of Shewan hegemony. Attempts by British officers to persuade church dignitaries, including Abune Markos, that the Church should not interfere with politics — as it was supposed it did not in Britain — were frequent. The clerics listened courteously, but ignored such advice, which while good intentioned perhaps, was in its way a typical product of the insularity and mental inflexibility demonstrated by some Britons in Africa. Later the Unionist movement received quite overt financial assistance from representatives of the Ethiopian government, but their measure of control over party policies has been exaggerated. Indeed their lack of it was to lead to protracted struggle after the British left.

There was considerable sympathy for the view that Eritrea should be independent from Shewa, as well as from Italy and Britian, united perhaps with Tigrai, some argued, under the possible but unsolicited leadership of Seyoum Mangasha. This was argued by Tesemma Asberom (who was considered pro-Italian and whom the Ethiopians wished to apprehend) and his son Abraha, for example. These two were later given titles by the British who may well have hoped to retain both an interest in any Tigrai-Eritrea state which might emerge. They also hoped for the eventual transfer of certain Muslim parts of western Eritrea to the Sudan which at that time they also ruled. The relevant archive for this period is now open for study.

Brigadier Longrigg, a British chief administrator of Eritrea, has written that:

> once off the coptic (sic) highlands it is certain that no considerable element whatsoever of the population desires a close connection with the Ethiopian empire.

Those areas were largely Muslim and they did soon express a desire — which has been consistent — for complete independence. They acted through political organisations. Divisions within Eritrea were not, however, at all simple. Even if the British only partially understood them they were not unaware of new levels of political consciousness and mounting tension. A British memorandum dated 28 June 1941, observed:

> An important political problem the Italians create lies in the irritation (this is one man's word for another man's nationalism) they cause the native populace, coupled with the necessity for our recognising Italian sovereignty, temporarily in abeyance, in a country in which Italian prestige has suffered severely in the eyes of the native population, which vastly outnumbers the Italians.

and warned:

> Since the Italians are to a large extent dependent on the native for supplies, and since the Italians have the lion's share of capital and commerce, relations between the two races must not be allowed to become too bad. As time passes their relationship may improve of itself, but as long as Italians continue to exercise executive authority over natives, or until the natives see that the British are going to adopt more sympathetic administrative measures, with which intention they are credited, this improvement will be uncertain in many parts of the country.

"What do we want?", one British administrator enquired rhetorically, and continued:

> It is the duty of the British Administration in Eritrea to administer the country with the minimum demands for military assistance and

shipping, and to exercise a prudent expenditure of sterling. At present soldiers are far more valuable than money in the Middle East.

Our leniency towards the Italians must be dictated by our own interests, and we are not here to strive after a native Utopia, although our administration should not be so open to criticism that it adversely affects British prestige in neighbouring countries . . .

It was recognised that goodwill on the part of the Eritrean intelligentsia was fast running out and there was soon a relapse into the usual colonial (and neo-colonial) argument 'that some foreigner must be behind' every popular expression of discontent:

The economic aspect of the native problem is more serious and might have an appreciable effect on security. If the natives are to have hard times economically it is essential that the political atmosphere should be fair.

The foreign elements are small and on the whole a political nuisance . . . They will accentuate the political pendulum against the Italians, possibly by supporting the more extravagant native claims.

The Eritreans did get their message across — but that is a different matter from having something done as a result. Not long afterwards the frustration felt by Eritrea's workers was noted:

They complain we have maintained the prestige of the whites and that things are no better than before. They claim we have cheated them with our promises and have apparently forgotten how courageously they fought against the Italians at Keren and elsewhere when we came to liberate them.

In Massawa, especially where the Italians were dependent on *native labour,* there is much discontent owing to unemployment and scarcity of food. *Trouble is to be expected from this quarter* unless something is done for this considerable native community. (my emphasis)

It has been observed how vital it is to grasp the role of the Eritrean working class in comprehending the successes — and historians may one day also conclude, some of the failures — of modern Eritrean nationalism. But let us employ the methodology Nkrumah advocated and go to 'the writings of Eritreans themselves'.

In the context of the 'African Revolution', Eritrea's opinion formers demonstrated a very advanced level of political consciousness, comparable with that among South African workers or Egyptians if one includes north Africa. An Eritrean appeal to the British, dated 12 December 1941, significantly condemns the Italians for the typical colonial claim that the country was without history and for not wanting the 'tribes to unite.' The Italians, it was asserted, 'needed the Eritreans purely as soldiers . . . (but) to liberate the Eritrean people it was necessary to bring Eritreans into the government'.

By 26 February 1942, the tone had become more critical:

> The people of Eritrea are not improving their position . . . Perhaps
> the white race will never recognise the negro but will always treat
> him in the manner desired by the white Italians . . .
> The Eritreans did everything possible to demonstrate to the
> Italians that they answered menace with rebellion. They fought
> against them and lent their support to Britain saying, "Hurrah and
> Hurrah for England".

> The solidarity of the black people will surely unite the Eritreans
> who have already revolted against the Governor. When an Eritrean
> was killed by an Italian captain of the carabinieri one Italian was
> condemned to nine months imprisonment yet immediately after-
> wards when an old Italian was killed in Hamasien four or five Eritreans
> were shot to avenge his death.
> As a result crimes by Italians against Eritreans are increasing
> from day to day. The British political officers are far too tolerant
> towards the Italians and give them ridiculously light punishments for
> grave crimes.
> More important than a battle, say the Eritreans, will eventually
> be the disorders and revolts of the black against the white race,
> which will grow in intensity, and will give rise to political results.
> There is a need to study Pan-African agitation, which aims
> almost at a war of all the non-whites. (Already for two years the
> League of the Coloured People against Oppression and Imperialism
> has met at a Congress). Such action must resemble Pan-Asiatic propa-
> ganda . . .

At this point, in disillusion the writer develops fantasies about the
possibility of true liberation at the hands of the Japanese:

> The only friend of the black races was England, but even the
> English favour the Italians. What remains? The Japanese.
>   . . . The Eritrean used to believe in the English. When they did
> not know and had never seen them, they loved them. But now they
> have seen their methods many Eritreans have lost faith in the English.

Was this much different from the findings of Lord Pearce in Zimbabwe
thirty years later? But I urged also collation and comparison of sources.
What were the British saying? One self-satisfied report dated April
1943, comments:

> The behaviour of the native population continues to be good.
> Prices are high, but within reach of most urban natives, though in
> the country there are few buyers at the present price for the stocks
> held by the Administration.
>   In Asmara about 200 members of the so-called Eritrean Com-
> mittee is functioning with the safe-guarding of Eritrean interests as
> its main object. At the request of this Committee an Eritrean Council
> has been set up to voice native opinion. The formation of this Coun-
> cil has caused a favourable impression and there are *no indications*

at present of Eritrean Nationalism or of sympathy with Abyssinian Irredentism.

That last point is interesting. As British military administrators were replaced by ex-colonial service officials, the level of understanding diminished. But even so, some at least of the intrigues of the restored government in Addis Ababa were known:

> The Abuna Marcos is an intriguer whose main object is to exploit the present state of affairs in Eritrea to his own advantage. His intrigues have not met with much encouragement at our hands, and he is therefore flirting at present both with the Italians and with the Emperor. What *little irrendentism there is in Asmara* (my emphasis but this is significant) undoubtedly emanates from his entourage, and he is a man to be carefully watched and handled. Clever and unscrupulous, he wields a considerable influence among the superstitious and priest-ridden peasants.

In fact, as stated above, the Abuna was reportedly rebuked on 27 February 1943, and told to confine himself to 'religious affairs'.

But the British were losing touch in a manner, it seems to me, they always did when nationalism in the colonies became a real force. Anyone who has read colonial archives comes to anticipate that old colonial adage 'only a handful of agitators'. (Actually it is neo-colonial too — read most reports on student unrest in independent Africa.) Miss Pankhurst, whose research brought the above reports to light, cites a British Administration report for the middle of April 1942, describing the 'politically minded' section of the community as 'very small' and mainly composed of 'a number of disgruntled ex-Government employees, a few leading merchants and a small number of Coptic priests.' The vast majority of the people, it declared, was 'exclusively concerned with the non-too-easy problem of how to earn the daily bread.' All this is reminiscent of such crass statements, for example, as that published by the administrative authority of Tanganyika, against Julius Nyerere and Tanu after the latter's visit to the United Nations in 1958, which denied that they were in any way representative of their people.

The writings even of staunch foreign supporters of union with Ethiopia, if carefully examined, may thus be found to illustrate Eritrean reservations on that issue. Sylvia Pankhurst describes a visit by Brigadier Longrigg to Addi Caieh where he

> called together the representatives of the people and invited them to express their views on the future of Eritrea, promising to forward their views to London. The Chiefs were reluctant to express their true desire, . . . (that is the fact — what follows is the interpretation) which was reunion to Ethiopia. They feared that by answering frankly they might incur the anger of the Brigadier, whose opposition to the reunion cause had already been disclosed . . .

(then more facts are revealed:)

. . . The Chiefs of Addi Caieh decided to answer with caution, verbally at that time and afterwards in writing. They averred that they represented but a small part of Eritrea and could not, therefore, reply to so important a question without consulting other districts. They informed the Chiefs of Asmara of what Brigadier Longrigg had said, and showed them their written reply to him. The Asmara Chiefs considered they must take action in reply to Brigadier Longrigg's proposal. As meetings were prohibited under the British order that no more than three persons might assemble, they decided to meet in small groups in various houses to discuss the future and to take in this way a plebiscite wherein all could vote as they thought best.*

Close scrutiny reveals that these Eritrean Chiefs were firm believers in the democratic principle and they certainly displayed a high level of political acrumen. Nor, in fact, did they declare for 'union' or federation,

The Role of the United Nations

Meantime, however, it was not aspirations of the natural leaders of the people which were to guide Eritrea into the second half of the twentieth century, but a resolution of the United Nations General Assembly, for the great powers could not agree. Nor indeed were their individual attitudes at all consistent. They regarded Italy's former colonies as mere pawns in a wider diplomacy. The Soviet Union, for example, at first supported the return of her former colonies to Italy, but after the defeat of the Communist Party in the Italian General Election of April 1948 she completely reversed her attitude, and was not alone in such 'adjustments'. The communist bloc did not see their volte-face as being inconsistent. The Ukraine delegate said his government 'had hoped the former Italian colonies might be placed under the administration of a democratic Italy freed from fascism.' The present government of Italy, however, had 'delivered that country bound hand and foot into the hands of the capitalists.' His government had, therefore, 'realised the impossibility of allowing Italy to administer any of its former colonies'.

Political pressures on the administering power — the British government — were many and varied. For example, the *Catholic Herald* urged the return of her former colonies to Italy while, as had been pointed out, Sylvia Pankhurst, through *New Times* and *Ethiopia News*, Jomo Kenyatta and others fought to keep claims by Ethiopia before the public. Meantime there was no plebiscite in Eritrea. More significant, in the event, was secret diplomacy. It is now clear from Senate enquiries, Ethiopian revolutionary court proceedings and the writings of some of those involved, that the United States entered into

* Quotations are from S. Pankhurst, *Ethiopia and Eritrea* (London, 1953) passim.

agreements with Emperor Haile Sellassie conditioned by other priorities, but which proved catastrophic to the cause of Eritrean freedom and independence. Indeed, all aspects of the international struggles which preceded the eventual granting to Italy in 1949 of a ten-year United Nations Trusteeship over her former Somaliland colony, in the face of Ethiopian objection — curiously citing the principle of self-determination — to the 1952 Federation of Eritrea with Ethiopia, were protracted and complex.

All I have time to do here is to note that after eleven years of British administration and mounting political pressure both inside and outside Eritrea, the General Assembly of the United Nations resolved on 2 December 1950, by 46 votes to 10, that Eritrea should 'constitute an autonomous unit federated with Ethiopia under the sovereignty of the Ethiopian crown'. The next contribution will take up the story and analyse the tragic sequence and the failure of not only Ethiopia, but the whole world community to stand by the commitments that were made.

From British Rule to Federation and Annexation

Bereket Habte Selassie

HISTORICAL BACKGROUND

The history of Eritrea is too long and complex to be summarized here, but the main outline may be traced in terms of the persistent themes which have characterized it. To begin with, the territory known as Eritrea today has been the object of many waves of colonizing adventures for some three thousand years.

Eritrea today has an area of approximately 119,000 square kilometres, and a population of over three million. The territory stretches for some 800 kms along the Red Sea Coast — its longest border — and is bordered in the north and west by the Sudan, and in the south by Ethiopia and Djibouti. The topography is a mixture of the mountainous central and northern highlands, with an escarpment descending to the western plains of Barka with its rich soils, and the arid eastern Afar region which provides for little livelihood or commerce.

Some of the earlier colonizers came as peaceful settlers, migrating from across the Red Sea, occupying the coastal areas first and moving gradually to the highlands where they found the climate more hospitable. Others came as conquerors. All were eventually absorbed by the more numerous Hamitic people, who nevertheless benefited from the higher technological skills of the immigrants. Population movements from the north, notably of the Beja people, wars and other causes disrupted peaceful development of the earlier settled inhabitants.

These earlier historical processes produced cultural and ethnic mixtures resulting in national groups with some distinct physionomic and cultural traits, which incidentally characterize the people of the Horn as a whole. The legacy of the Axumite civilization and of Nubia represent the richest land-marks of these historical processes. The most important legacy of the Axumite culture was the Geez Alphabet. The greater part of Eritrea formed part of the central region of the Axumite empire, together with the northern Ethiopian province of Tigrai.

Axum prospered and thrived on maritime trade with the outside world through the ancient port of Adulis — near Massawa. The Axumite rulers subjugated various peoples and incorporated them into their empire which at its zenith stretched as far south as the northern fringe of the Semien Mountains south of Tigrai, and as far north/west as

Nubia, in present day Sudan. The decline of external trade came about with the rise of Islam and the occupation of the Red Sea Coast by Arab forces in 640 AD. Internal political dissention and the advent of the Bejas from the North were further causes for the demise of an empire which had already shrunk in size in consequence of the loss of external trade. The Axumite kingdom, which had been converted to Christianity by Syrian missionaries in the 4th century, finally broke up towards the end of the 9th century AD[1].

During the centuries that followed the break up of the Axumite empire several states rose and fell around the area of Axum. It must be noted, in passing, that present day Ethiopia, which is a creation of Menelik's imperial expansion in the 1880's and 1890's, in no way corresponds to the ancient Axumite kingdom, contrary to the claim of some Ethiopians!

Parts of northern Ethiopia (present day Tigrai) and the Eritrean highland plateau formed the core of the Axumite State. Similarly parts of Western Eritrea were the subject of invasion and conquests from neighbouring nations throughout history. The reverse is also true, in that some of the north-western Eritrean ethnic groups have crossed over to the Sudan.

It is known, for example, that after the break up of Axum the Bejas invaded Eritrea and maintained their rule over the Eritrean highlands until the end of the 13th century.[2] This represents a period of four centuries after the fall of Axum, during which no Abyssinian[3] king ruled over any part of Eritrea. In fact there was no such (Abyssinian) rule until after the 15th century, when historical records reveal inter-mittent Abyssinian incursions and tenuous rule over parts of Eritrea, which by then begins to bear the name of Medri Bahri (Land of the Sea). The people of Medri Bahri — essentially the highland areas — never accepted the rule of Abyssinian kings, be they Amhara kings from Gondar or Tigreans from neighbouring Tigrai. There was continuous resistance, even at the height of their subjugation, as witness the rebel-lion of Woldemicael of Hamasien, and Bahta Hagos of Akele-Guzai.[4]

The critical importance of geography in defining national frontiers or in imposing limits on conquests becomes evident when account is taken of the great physical divide exerted by the Semien mountain ranges reaching north to Adoa, as well as the Tekeze valley. These geo-graphical factors, added to the distance in time after the fall of Axum, explain the specific nationalist features of the Eritrean highland people and the tenacity of their resistance to Abyssinian attempts to rule over them.

On the Western front also, similar developments can in part be ex-plained in these terms. After the advent of the Funj kingdom in the Sudan (1504-1821) we see a historic dividing line between Sudan and Eritrea. The mountainous fringe which rises steeply from the eastern plains of the Sudan exerted a historic limit to the expansion of the Funj empire, thus establishing a national frontier with Eritrea. On both fronts, the people of the area, when not at war with each other, maintained peaceful relations through some key mountain passes, trading and learning from each other.

The rise of Islam, followed by the advent of the Ottoman Turks critically affected the history of Eritrea as it did other parts of the region. The Ottoman Turks occupied the coastal region in 1557, effectively cutting off the highland interior from the world outside. In the face of this plight the central highlands of Eritrea and the neighbouring northern Abyssinian regions maintained links sometimes of mutual benefit, often times characterized by an Abyssinian penchant for expansion and dominion and Eritrean resistance. The Orthodox Church of Abyssinia, which was under the Egyptian Coptic Church, played a role in attempts to forge a highland Christian Kingdom united against the Islamic Turkish rule.

In 1872, after over three hundred years of Turkish hegemony over the region, Egypt made a bid for power as regional successor to the Ottoman Turks. Turkish hegemony had not penetrated the highland areas of Eritrea. The Egyptians, with British encouragement, made an attempt to do what the Turks had failed to do in three hundred years. With British help, the Egyptians secured the transfer of all Turkish possessions in Eritrea through a treaty in 1875. Spurred on by the success of this diplomatic coup, the Egyptians embarked upon a military adventure which proved to be disastrous and costly. They were defeated in a series of battles east of Massawa, at the hands of the Eritreans and their Tigrean allies.

British motives to set Egypt upon such an adventure stemmed from a desire to keep the French out of the area. The opening of the Suez Canal in 1869 had introduced European colonial interest into the region, as a vital strategic area. Egypt used its role as a junior partner in the Anglo-Egyptian condominium over the Sudan to carve out a sphere of interest for itself. But the condominium faced a grave threat in the rise of Mahdism in the Sudan which resulted in the overthrow of the condominium and the establishment of the Mahdist State, which lasted until 1898. While the Mahdist revolt shook the Anglo-Egyptian hegemony over the Sudan, Eritrea fell under Italian colonial rule[5].

The Eritrean people's sense of entrapment and isolation is one of the major themes of their history, as succeeding colonial powers encircled them and occupied their land. Herein lies the deep root of Eritrean nationalism. Modern Eritrean nationalism, of course, manifested itself in many forms during and immediately after Italian colonial rule. And it continues to do so, this time in a more organised form, as will be seen below. But it cannot be overemphasised that Eritrean nationalism is not a new phenomenon. It is historically rooted in the common struggle of the Eritrean people against diverse forms of alien rule — a point many Ethiopians (even progressive Ethiopians) do not sufficiently appreciate, or want to understand.

IMPERIALIST INTRIGUES AND THE NATIONAL RESISTANCE MOVEMENT

There is a remarkable story connected with modern Eritrean nationalism which is not widely known. It involves British intrigues in the 1940s to partition Eritrea along ethno-religious lines — the western part to be added to the Anglo-Egyptian Sudan, and the highlands and eastern part to be given to their newly adopted protegé, emperor Haile Selassie. This story is remarkable on two counts. First, it shows the brazen attempt to use ethnic politics as a basis for determining the destiny of a nation by a colonial power, notorious for creating artificial boundaries throughout its colonial empires, in reckless disregard of divided nations and families. Second, and more important, the response of the Eritrean people was swift, decisive and uncompromising in opposing the partition plan.[6] It was the first dramatic manifestation of a united Eritrean nationalist sentiment in modern times, and a harbinger of more struggle to come. Previously, such massive demonstration of nationalist sentiment was suppressed by successive colonial regimes;[7] but it was alive, smouldering beneath the calm exterior of the colonial legal order.

British Rule (1941-1952)

The advent of British rule brought with it new hopes for the Eritrean people. The sinewy and sullen British who took the position of the Italians as the new colonial masters easily established their authority. They were able to do this without resistance because they were welcomed as liberators. The Eritrean people were given pledges that if they helped to defeat the Italians, the British would help them to exercise their right of self-determination.[8] Even before the beginning of hostilities with Italy, Eritreans looked to the British for help, particularly after the advent of Mussolini. Some of the influential members of the Eritrean intelligentsia, mostly mission-educated, had maintained contacts with the British in the Sudan.

After the outbreak of hostilities, British royal air force planes dropped leaflets, promising freedom to Eritrea, thus stimulating suppressed nationalist aspirations for self-determination. The leaflets were a mild beginning of a more intense process of political agitation which followed later.

As it became clear that the British would not honour their pledge, political agitation began to take more organised and militant forms. Political agitation was made possible because the British permitted a measure of freedom of speech and association. The British also established an active press and information service which published and broadcast in English, Tigrinya and Arabic, news on the progress of war in Europe and other issues. These two parallel developments spawned prominent political activists and commentators, some of whom would be destined to play important roles in the Eritrean national political struggle.

The most celebrated among these people was Wolde-Ab Wolde-Mariam, whose column commenting on Eritrea's future was widely read. Every issue of the meagre publication was consumed avidly, read and reread, discussed and debated in the cities and large villages. This process galvanised mass political opinion, especially in the urban centres, and helped raise the awareness of the Eritrean masses. It partly explains the election of Wolde-Ab as the president of the Eritrean Trade Union of Workers, which would play a critical role at a later phase of the Eritrean struggle.

The years of British rule of Eritrea thus saw the emergence of organised political groups, with a rising political consciousness among the Eritrean masses. The formation of different political groups had the effect of clarifying the issues surrounding the status and future of Eritrea. By the end of 1945 the political tendencies crystalised as political 'parties'; the Eritrean Independence Party led by Wolde-Ab, the Rabita Al Islamia led by Ibrahim Sultan, and the Unionist Party led by Tedla Bairu, were the principal formations.

The backstage intrigues of interested powers is an inseparable part of the story of the formation and fortune of these parties and of the careers of their leading personalities. Bribery and terror were among the principle methods used by the powers. Haile Selassie's government used the Ethiopian Orthodox Church as a political weapon, dividing Eritreans along religious lines.

Mass consciousness and participation was not limited to the urban centres. Village schools were mushrooming, in addition to those in the cities, under a crash programme organised and directed by an energetic British education officer. This produced in rapid succession crops of literate youngsters who helped in the spread of political education through daily reading of newspaper articles to parents. In this way, ideas and opinions were communicated effectively, and names like Wolde-Ab became household words together with what they stood for.

News of local political events could not be analysed outside the context of the international reality of the time. Some of the most relevant world events were reported and discussed as part of the political struggle. A chronology of the principal events surrounding the disposal of the ex-Italian colonies will help us to put the local political scene at that time in its larger historical perspective.

Immediately after the end of the war the Allied Powers held the Paris Peace Conference in June 1946, at which Italy formally renounced all her rights to Libya, Eritrea and Italian Somaliland. The Treaty of Paris stipulated that the final disposal of the ex-Italian territories would be determined by agreement among France, Great Britain, the United States of America and the USSR. In the event of a failure to agree among the 'Big Four' within a year, the matter would be submitted to the United Nations.[9]

In November 1947, a commission of inquiry was established with terms of reference to visit the three territories and to report on the political situation. The commission submitted a report in May 1948, but there was no basis on which the Big Powers could agree. The matter was therefore placed before the United Nations in April 1949. It was to this (third) session of the United Nations that the infamous Bevin-Sforza plan was submitted. According to the play Libya was to be divided into three parts to be ruled (one each) by the British, the French and the Italians, under a 'trusteeship', and Italian Somaliland was to be administered under Italian trusteeship, while Eritrea would be partitioned between the Sudan and Ethiopia along the lines mentioned earlier. The whole scheme collapsed, once more failing to provide a solution to the three territories.

At the 4th Session of the United Nations the future of Libya and Italian Somaliland was decided – Libya to be granted independence by January 1952, and Somalia to be under a ten-year Italian trusteeship after which it would be independent.[10] The United Nations failed to reach agreement on Eritrea. It therefore decided to send a second commission of inquiry, composed of five members – Burma, Guatemala, Norway, Pakistan and South Africa.

The Commission presented its findings on June 28, 1949 as follows: the majority consisting of Burma, Norway and South Africa recommended a close association of Eritrea with Ethiopia; Burma and South Africa proposed federation with Ethiopia under Ethiopian sovereignty, while Norway recommended unconditional union with Ethiopia. The minority report of Guatemala and Pakistan recommended a United Nations trusteeship over Eritrea for ten years, after which Eritrea would become independent. Both majority and minority reports opposed partition, thus fairly and accurately reflecting Eritrean sentiments.

This last point involves perhaps the only matter on which the Eritrean peoples' views were heard and fairly represented, despite British machinations to make partition a reality. The majority report succumbed to such machinations and misguided information, when it concluded, for example, that Eritrea was not capable of establishing a viable economy – a factor which it considered of decisive importance in reaching its decision. Such a conclusion, which flies in the face of the facts, was influenced by the opinions of the 'Administering Power', which had control of all economic and other data on Eritrea. The opinion of the British on this matter was revealed by the remarks of the British delegate to the United Nations in the debate in the Ad Hoc Political Committee.

Britain, as the Administering Power had all the leverage to influence the outcome of events on the Eritrean question. After several attempts at partition, the British threw their lot in support of the Ethiopian claim, at the behest of the United States of America. Emperor Haile Selassie made his claims on Eritrea both on economic and on baseless historical grounds. The United States, which emerged as the dominant economic and military power after World War II, was now getting involved in the Korean war. When the Korean war broke out on 25 June 1950, Britain was a weakened imperial power, with its domestic economy in a shambles and a diminishing international role.

The debate on the divided report of the Commission of Inquiry on Eritrea took place in a political atmosphere dominated by the Korean war. The Eritrean question was seen in a new light by an expanding American imperialist role, which was fast replacing the British role in many areas of the world. Aklilu Habtewold who was Ethiopian minister of foreign affairs at the time has boastfully claimed since then that Haile Selassie's diplomacy exploited the cold war by openly staking the future and fortune of Ethiopia on the side of western powers led by the United States, in return for a 'deal' on Eritrea.[11]

Ethiopia's commitment on the side of the West was fulfilled in more ways than one. Haile Selassie sent a battalion of his well trained Imperial Bodyguard to fight on the US side in the Korean war. Another dramatic illustration of the changing roles in the imperial game showing the United States to be the ascendant imperialist power was the grant to the US of the Kagnew communications base near Asmara.[12] Before the British handover of Eritrea in 1952, the United States and Emperor Haile Selassie signed a secret mutual defence pact lasting for twenty-five years, under which the United States 'leased' the Kagnew base, and Haile Selassie would obtain military and other assistance.

Some time before the treaty was signed, Haile Selassie had placed himself at the disposal of the United States which in return manoeuvred the United Nations to push for a 'federal' solution for Eritrea. This is the background against which United Nations Resolution 390 A (v) was passed on 2 December 1950 proposing that Eritrea be constituted as an autonomous unit to be federated with Ethiopia under the sovereignty of the Ethiopian Crown. This was clearly in violation of the United Nations Charter and contrary to the wishes of the Eritrean people for self-determination.[13]

From Federation to Annexation (1952-1962)

The United Nations Resolution provided for an autonomous Eritrean government with legislative, executive and judicial powers over domestic affairs, with matters of defence, foreign affairs, currency and finance, foreign and interstate trade and communications falling under 'federal' (or Ethiopian) jurisdiction. In the interim period between December 1950 and September 1952 a United Nations Commissioner would be appointed to prepare a draft constitution for Eritrea and submit it to an Eritrean Assembly to be convened by the British Administering Authority.

It should be noted here that the Soviet Union, along with nine other members of the United Nations, opposed the 'federal' solution, proposing instead complete independence for Eritrea in accordance with the provisions of the U.N. Charter. The preamble of the Resolution which set out the supposed rationale is a travesty of justice. It reads, inter alia:

> Taking into consideration (a) the wishes and welfare of the inhabitants of Eritrea, including the views of the various racial, religious and political groups of the provinces of the territory and the capacity of the people for self-government; (b) the interests of peace and security in East Africa; (c) the rights and claims of Ethiopia based on geographical, historical, ethnic or economic reasons, including in particular Ethiopia's legitimate need for adequate access to the sea. . . Desiring that this association (of Eritrea with Ethiopia) assures to the inhabitants of Eritrea the *fullest respect and safeguards for their institutuions, traditions, religions and languages,* as well as the widest possible measure of self-government . . . (my italics)

The inconsistency inherent in this legal mumbo-jumbo is evident. How can 'the interests of peace' be secured when a basic condition has been denied, i.e. the *exercise* of the right of self-determination of the people, which right the United Nations arrogated to itself? How could a World Tribunal that took into consideration 'the wishes and welfare of the inhabitants of Eritrea' arrive at a decision which denied these wishes? Was it necessary to fabricate (or to endorse the Ethiopian fabrication of) 'historical reasons' in order to advance the economic interests of Ethiopia? Was Ethiopia's 'legitimate' need for adequate access to the sea in itself sufficient to cause the denial of the right to self-determination to the Eritrean people? Ethiopia is not, after all, the only nation which has a need for access to the sea.

The real reason of course lies elsewhere, and is not far to seek. John Foster Dulles, the then American Secretary of State, put it bluntly. Speaking before the United Nations Security Council in 1952, he said:

> From the point of view of justice, the opinions of the Eritrean people must receive consideration. Nevertheless the strategic interest of the United States in the Red Sea basin and considerations of security and world peace make it necessary that the country has to be linked with our ally, Ethiopia.[14]

The phrasing of Dulles' statement is significant. The word 'nevertheless' coming as it does after the sentence which recognizes the right of the Eritrean people, reveals beyond question that the United States (and hence the United Nations body) knew the wishes of the Eritrean people to be decisively for independence. The unqualified wish of the Eritrea people is juxtaposed against U.S. imperialist interests and those of its new found ally.

The Eritrean people were thus launched upon a new form of colonial rule under the guise of a federation. The United Nations Commissioner, Anze Matienzo, who was responsible for drafting the Eritrean Constitution spent many weeks negotiating with the Emperor and members of his government on some of the provisions of the draft constitution. The chief obstacle was the fact that the emperor's government was a semi-feudal one with no democratic pretensions, whereas the Eritrean constitution was of bourgeois democratic inspiration.

Anze Matienzo's formula for resolving this constitutional anomaly was to suggest that Ethiopia should revise its semi-feudal constitution (of 1931) and up-date it with some democratic trappings. This was the origin of the Revised Constitution of 1955. Matienzo's democratic conscience, such as it was, must have constantly pricked him in view of his knowledge that politically Eritrea was a much more developed country than Ethiopia, and that a democratic society was forcibly wedded to a feudal autocracy, in a lopsided federal scheme of unequal partnership with no 'neutral' arbiter. Perhaps this explains the interesting paragraph in his final report in which he wrote:

. . . it does not follow that the United Nations would no longer have any right to deal with the question. The United Nations Resolution on Eritrea would remain an international instrument and, if violated, the General Assembly could be seized of the matter.[15]

As it happened, the Resolution was violated almost immediately after the Federation was put into effect. Matienzo's cautionary remarks might be seen as prophetic, but for the fact that they were made by a man who knew the intentions and predictions of the Ethiopian government. The Emperor's spies and saboteurs were conducting smear campaigns and acts of terror against leading Eritrean personalities deep in Eritrean territory with British knowledge. Anze Matienzo had occasion to hear petitions from aggrieved Eritreans and thus gained a clear insight into the unsatisfied ambitions of the emperor.

At the international level, during the final debates of the General Assembly before the vote of 2 December 1950, Aklilu Habtewold after opposing the federal solution had finally accepted it but gave hints of such ambitions, when he declared that the federal solution was accepted by Ethiopia only 'in the spirit of compromise.' From the first moment after the British left, the emperor's government was clearly bent on violating the federal arrangements, and annexing Eritrea. The emperor's representative set out systematically to undermine the democratic principles of the Eritrean constitution and to put the Eritrean government under his control.

The Eritrean government was headed by Tedla Bairu, a leading member of the pro-Ethiopian Unionist Party. And now he was at logger heads with Andargachew, the emperor's representative in the first years of the federation. Tedla made some efforts to resist Andargachew's encroach-

ment on his domestic jurisdiction, both in the political as in the economic domain. The paradoxical drama of a democratically elected Chief
Executive being subverted by the representative of a feudal autocracy
was eventually resolved by the resignation of Tedla, followed by the
president of the Legislative Assembly.[16] Even as the battle was being
lost politically, the Eritrean attorney general (a British National) continued to engage in futile legal battles in the 'federal courts', in an
effort to check the encroachment.

Meanwhile Andargachew replaced Tedla with Asfaha, a trusted
Unionist and a former faithful servant of Italian colonial rulers. Asfaha
began to dismantle what was left of the autonomous institutions of
Eritrea, by placing Unionist cronies in key positions throughout the
administration. The Legislative Assembly was controlled by another
Unionist, Dimetros, an Orthodox cleric with Rasputinian proclivities.
Together Asfaha and Dimetros, under the direction of Andargachew,
and with the active agency of the police force, systematically terrorised
the people into submission or acquiescence. A Preventive Detention
Law, which Tedla had decreed, was used ruthlessly and extensively.

At the same time Andargachew entered into numerous joint ventures
with foreign and local businessmen, and thus presided over the rise of
a new bourgeoisie which ruthlessly acquired wealth and secured control
over vital economic institutions of Eritrea. This small but powerful
bourgeoisie formed the nucleus of a larger satellite of callaborators who
were brought by small handouts of government positions, land grants or
other emoluments – all with the emperor's blessing.

The role of the emporor's representative in terms of the federal
arrangements was meant to be mainly symbolic – to promulgate legislation and read imperial speeches or messages. The only substantive
legal power he possessed was his right to return to the Eritrean Assembly
legislation which he considered to encroach on federal (Ethiopian)
jurisdiction. But Andargachew saw his role as being much more than
that, and the emperor fully backed him in all his campaigns to break
Eritrea's national will and violate the terms of the United Nations
Resolution. Andargachew made the imperial intention explicit in a
speech he made to the Eritrean Assembly on 22 March 1955 in which
he said:

> There is no internal or external affairs, as far as the office of His
> Imperial Majesty's Representative is concerned, and there will be
> none in the future. The affairs of Eritrea concern Ethiopia as a
> whole and the Emperor.

Tedla's resignation came four months after this statement. All other
critics and leaders of the political opposition had either been jailed
or sent into exile. The stage was set for the final coup de grace to abolish the federation. The emperor decided to postpone this and bide his
time in the face of growing mass protests spear-headed by students,

workers and intellectuals.

The Eritrean masses were undergoing severe economic and social strains. The Emperor's government closed several industries and moved them to Addis Ababa, instructing their (foreign) owners to do so on pain of confiscation and expulsion from the country. The aim was two-fold: to weaken Eritrea economically and retroactively prove their point about its non-viability as an economy; secondly to strike at Eritrean labour which was an organized and effective national political force. These measures drove many thousands of Eritreans out of Eritrea to seek employment elsewhere, but they did not break the backbone of organised labour. The emperor had also long coveted Eritrean skilled manpower of which he now had an excess.

The emperor's desire was not limited to skilled manpower. It included access to the sea and rich mineral resources of which he was well informed. All of his ambitions agreed with US strategic interests. No wonder then that the pleas and protests made by the Eritrean exiled opposition leadership at the United Nations fell on deaf ears.

In Eritrea the continued violation of democratic human rights led to growing mass protests and demonstrations. The internal process was aided by external broadcasts made by some of the exiled opposition leaders like Wolde-Ab. Wolde-Ab in particular started a series of daily broadcasts from Cairo in late 1955 lasting only for a few months, which fanned the nationalist flames — or rather the embers — buried beneath the ashes of police terror and intimidation. The protests began taking massive organized forms. Throughout 1956 students intermittently boycotted classes, and in 1957 took to the streets after Tigrinya and Arabic were dropped as official languages and replaced by Amharic, the official Ethiopian language. This act not only violated the express provision of the UN Resolution,[17] but imposed a painful obstacle to the learning abilities of Eritrean children, setting them years behind. The effects are reflected some years later in secondary and university entrance examinations, which blocked the way to higher education for thousands of Eritreans. When students are affected everybody else is affected. Children brought back home with them the militancy of aggrieved youth and this fed an aggravated national sentiment.

These were the circumstances which provided the background for Wolde-Ab's effective broadcasts from Cairo. Haile Selassie was forced to make a deal with Gamal Abdel Nasser to back him in his bid to nationalise the Suez Canal in 1956, in exchange for stopping the broadcasts from Cairo. But the massage had been delivered loud and clear — and in a language which everybody understood and could remember.[18]

This was how the Eritrean Liberation Movement (ELM) was born. The masses: students, labour and intellectuals in particular created it; and dedicated leaders like Wolde-Ab helped to inspire and instruct its earlier stages. It had two principal centres: one situated in the highlands with its nucleus in Asmara, and the other in the lowlands with exiled

Eritreans living in the Sudan providing inspirational source. The two centres created various means of contact, including sports and other youth activities, but they were not organisationally linked. School teachers, students and other petty bourgeois intellectuals plus small tradesmen were the main sources of its recruitment. Its organisational laxity and lack of a clear political programme were its main handicaps, which eventually led to its collapse, but not before it had prepared the ground for the next stage of the struggle. Its highland version was known in its last phase as Mahber Shewate (the committee of seven), a cellular underground organisation, organized in the urban centres.[19] Its lowland version was known as Harakat Atahrir Al Eritrea (the Eritrean Liberation Movement), or simply Haraka.

This movement was too much handicapped to carry out any systematic struggle against the reign of terror of a police state. After massive police raids and arrests were carried out on several occasions the movement was decapitated. The movement had carried the national struggle one stage forward and cleared the way for the only alternative left, i.e. a protracted and popularly based armed struggle organized in the country side. It is important to note that the Eritrean armed struggle was begun after the Eritrean people had tried all other possible means of resistance and failed.

The United Nations arrangement had provided a modicum of democratic rights from which the Eritrean people tried to benefit. But all to no avail. One of the most dramatic expressions of resistance through the exercise of such democratic rights was the general strike of the Eritrean trades unions organized in 1958. The unions had been officially banned, but they continued to exist underground. The strike and the demonstrations which accompanied it were emphatic proof of the Eritrean national will to resist the demolition of democratic rights and to continue the struggle. In that confrontation Asfaha, the chief executive, ordered his police to fire on demonstrators which left some 500 dead or wounded. It was the first trade union strike action and demonstration to be met with such a magnitude of repression in the modern history of Africa. That brutal act cast the die for a change in the form of the Eritrean struggle. After some two years, the armed struggle was declared with the birth of the Eritrean Liberation Front (ELF) in September 1961.

A little over a year later, on 14 November 1962 Haile Selassie annexed Eritrea with the tacit support of the United States. Not a murmur was heard in the United Nations. The details of how Haile Selassie prepared the ground for the final legal act of abrogation of the federation need not detain us here. Suffice it to say that after years of terror and intimidation the handpicked members of the Eritrean Assembly were placed under duress to accept a speech from the throne that the federation was dissolved. The House of Assembly was surrounded by the units of the Ethiopian armed forces and police, some of whom were present with their machine guns inside the building when the 'vote' was taken. Some members who dared protest and walked out were arrested and beaten up. The role of the Eritrean chief of police in this task was very important. He was rewarded for his services, first with the emperor's gold watch and a special hand gun, and later with his still unexplained murder, which Haile Selassie's media called suicide. The truth is that he had come to realize too late the crime he had committed against his people.

After removing the formal obstacles, the feudal regime of the emperor proceeded to replace Eritrean laws and institutions with its own semi-feudal laws and institutions which were alien to the Eritrean people. Not even the Italian colonial rulers had dared to strike at the root of native law and custom. To back up this rapid violation the Ethiopian army of occupation was increased and spread around the country, with United States and Israeli help. The Eritrean people were thus left with no alternative but to resort to armed struggle.

Trevaskis who was political secretary of the British administration in Eritrea knew of Ethiopia's ambitions. He wrote in his book in 1960:

> The temptation to subject Eritrea firmly under her control will always be great. Should she try to do so, she will risk Eritrean discontent and eventual revolt, which, with foreign sympathy and support, might well disrupt both Eritrea and Ethiopia herself.[20]

CONCLUSION

The foregoing discussion has shown that Haile Selassie had begun to carry out his annexation plans long before the final illegal act of abrogation of the federation on 14 November 1962. The ELM must be seen as an expression of Eritrean resistance, partly in response to such annexationist ambitions, which has been clearly demonstrated in many spheres of Eritrean life. The declaration of the armed struggle in 1961 marks a definite stage in that resistance, although it is a break with the past forms of struggle.

War, it has been said, is the continuation of politics by other means. The declaration of the Eritrean war of liberation with the establishment of the ELF in September 1961 announced to a callous world community that the Eritrean people were driven to wage their political struggle the hard way. They were driven to take such a course of action after the violation of the United Nations Resolution went unsanctioned and virtually unnoticed, and after all peaceful means of protest had been tried and exhausted over a number of years.

Historically then we see three distinct phases in the modern Eritrean struggle, each marked by different forms. First there was the open political struggle waged by different groups during the time of British rule. Second, there was the underground movement culminating in the formation of the ELM. Third, came the armed struggle.

In terms of international law Haile Selassie's violation of the United Nations Resolution from the first moment constituted an illegal act which should have caused the General Assembly of the United Nations to be 'seized of the matter', as Matienzo had counselled. Repeated pleas made by Eritreans to the United Nations went unheaded. Legally, therefore, the violation of the Resolution as an international instrument gave the Eritrea people the right to use any and every available means to wage a struggle against a regime which by its own acts had become an occupying colonial regime. The Eritrean people were, by the same token, placed in a *status quo ante* — to a pre-1950 situation of a colonised people engaged in a struggle for self-determination and independence from colonial rule. This is why the Eritrean struggle involved a colonial question, and not one of secession.

In terms of international politics, the American alliance with Haile Selassie which had manoeuvred the United Nations into sacrificing the Eritrean people on the altar of imperialist games, now turned Ethiopia into an imperialist stooge. This was backed by a mutual defence pact signed in 1953, as noted above, and created a military and economic dependency relationship. Haile Selassie's violation of the United Nations Resolution was therefore tacitly supported by the United States. In short, Haile Selassie had turned Ethiopia into a neo-colony and Eritrea became a colony of a neo-colony. The Eritrean struggle thus became at once an anti-colonial and anti-imperialist struggle, as early as 1953, even though it was not articulated then in so many words.

The genesis and progress of the armed struggle, with all its internal contradictions, must be properly seen in the light of this reality and its ramifications. One of the ramifications of that reality was the Arab-Israeli conflict. The Unites States-Israeli alliance with Ethiopia, the historical and geographic links of Eritrea with the Arab world plus the support of the Eritrean cause by many Arab countries also made the Eritrean struggle an anti-Zionist struggle. An early EPLF document addresses this issue succintly thus:

> Eritrea is an African country with close ties with the Arab world, as it is strategically situated on the south-western flank of the Middle East.[21]

Without thoroughly digesting this political fact, one cannot understand the Eritrean Revolution's position in the fight against world imperialism.

Historically, the strategic factor has impinged on Eritrean politics, imposing constraints on the struggle to maintain or regain independence. In that long struggle some form of inter-dependence has alternated with autonomy and isolation. When Turko/Egyptian hegemony or European colonisation was the main threat, Eritreans sought alliance (and in some cases refuge) with their southern neighbours. When Ethiopian expansion was the threat, succour and/or alliance was sought elsewhere. In the last instance this is what happend after the US-backed Ethiopian occupation became a *fait accompli* in the 1950's. Every form of dependence has its price. It is partly as a result of the historic lessons learnt by the Eritrean people that the EPLF made self-reliance the corner-stone of its socio-economic policy. Friends of the Eritrean revolution marvel and rejoice at the miracle of self-reliance typified by the underground workshops in Sahel. They also lament, as we all do, the massive deployment of Soviet armoury to back an army of invasion. The whole world looks on as this David and Goliath type of spectacle begins its second year. The progressive world needs to pay serious attention, and react appropriately, to the war in Eritrea, because now for the first time in its history a socialist power has committed men and machines, and its prestige, to negate the cause of a revolution which it once supported as a just one.

References
1. See e.g. J.S. Trimingham *Islam in Ethiopia*, (Oxford University Press, London, 1952); G.K.N. Trevaskis, *Eritrea: a Colony in Transition, 1941-1952*, (Greenwood Press, Westport Connecticut, 1975); E. Ullendorf, *The Ethiopians*, (Oxford University Press, London, 1973).
2. See J.S. Trimingham. *op.cit.* pp.49-50.
3. The term 'Abyssinian' is used here to describe rulers representing the Amhara Kingdom which thrived first in the Shoan highlands and later (after the advent of Ahmed Gragne in the early 16th century) in Gondar.
4. For the resistance against Amhara rule see Almeida, *Some Records of Ethiopia, 1593-1646*, Series 2, Vol 107, (Haklyut Society), pp.182-184.
5. On Menelik's dealings with Italy see Carlo Rossetti, *Storia Diplomatica Dell' Ethiopia*, (Torina, 1910).
6. For the social and political effects of these acts see *In Defense of the Eritrean Revolution*, Association of Eritrean Students in North America, (New York, 1978), pp.40-41.
7. See Travaskis *op.cit.*, p.33. The native student was made to sing songs about the glory of Italy and to feel ashamed of his own history. He had to depend on the oral tradition told by the elders of his nation to have a sense of pride in his own history.
8. As many as 60,000 Eritreans were sent to Libya alone. See *In Defence of the Eritrean Revolution*, p.41.
9. Article 23 of the Treaty. See also paragraph 3 of Annex II.
10. See Resolution 289A (iv).
11. A written statement he submitted to the Commission of Enquiry established to investigate Emperor Haile Selassie's government in 1974.
12. 'Kagnew' was the name of the battalion which was sent to fight in Korea. It was also the nom de guerre of Ras Makonnen, Haile Selassie's father.
13. See Articles 1 and 55 of the Charter.
14. Market International Report, (Ethiopia- Summary), January 1977, quoted in Linda Heiden, 'The Eritrean Struggle for Independence', *Monthly Review*, July-August 1978, p.15.
15. United Nations Commissioner for Eritrea – Final Report. Chapter II. p.201.
16. The paradox of this relationship in constitutional terms is described by the eminent British professor of constitutional law, Ivor Jennings, see his *Approach to Independence*, (Oxford University Press, London, 1956).

17. Cf. the preamble of the UN Resolution, quoted above.
18. Wolde-Ab is a past master of the Tigrigna language equalled by few, both in spoken and written form. His use of apt proverbs and simple stories appealed to the masses. There were also broadcasts in Arabic made by others to good advantage.
19. The author was associated with the ELM in Addis Ababa.
20. Trevaskis *op.cit.*
21. 'The Historical Background of the (Eritrean) Civil War' – A statement issued by the EPLF on Dec. 4, 1972. See *Liberation*, Vol. II No.4., April/ May 1973.

PART II

THE NATURE OF THE
LIBERATION STRUGGLE

The wide-ranging victories of the Eritrean liberation movement had enabled a shift from guerilla warfare to open confrontation and the taking of all but a few towns. However, the Ethiopian forces had been able to break out of their encirclement around Asmara in late 1978 and take back many towns. This was made possible by Soviet military aid.

Connell's report published below, which was presented to the Symposium, is an eye-witness account of some of the major battles of this period and the EPLF's switch back to guerilla tactics. This forms Chapter 5.

In the period from early 1979, this is how the EPLF has responded to the continuing offensive against them. It is noteworthy that despite their heavy armoury and Soviet backing, the Ethiopians were still turned back and denied entry to the main EPLF base areas. What comes across is the EPLF view that although they expect the tide of battle may see-saw back and forth, their own struggle will certainly go on.

The second account (Ch. 6) offers a different perspective – of the towns that have been lost to the Ethiopians and the repression that has gone on in them. (Editors)

The Guerilla Struggle
Gerard Chaliand

Over the years the Eritrean People's Liberation Front has demonstrated an ability to sustain two mobilisational tasks which are crucial for the development of any effective national liberation movement: it has been able to build a strong organisation which has remained cohesive; and it has shown a capacity to generate cadres. This success in mobilisation represents a great achievement.

Years have in fact been spent mobilising in both Moslem and Christian areas. This solid preparatory work took place between 1974 and 1978 in Eritrea. Moreover, this was mobilisation of the people in both areas not on the strength of sloganising, as has been the case in some other countries, but by changing completely their conditions of life.

The Organisational Achievements of the EPLF

A key part of the mobilisation has been the elections to mass organisations in the villages, of women, youth and other groups. The EPLF has in fact succeeded especially in mobilising women. Great stress is placed on women's participation within the struggle. Within its own ranks there is a great proportion of women — perhaps 25% — which is a fantastic achievement considering these were very conservative societies.

The mobilisation has included other groups; younger people in the 15-18 years age group are organised. There has been the creation of a *militia*, consisting of both men and women, in the liberated areas. State-like structures have been set up at the village level and for liberated zones. These run *schools* for the old as well as the young, plus *health clinics* and other facilities. These bodies also work with the nomads to curb cattle disease. They operate *people's stores* where people go and buy at market prices the goods to meet their basic needs. *Cooperatives* meet about 60% of the food and other needs of the fighters.

The EPLF tries to be as self-sufficient as possible. It is important psychologically that they do not rely on outside help.

A very effective communications network has been developed. Their workshops are unique in Africa. They handle the repair of trucks, metal work, carpentry and joinery, textiles and radio repairs. Skilled manual work is the basis of all these operations. The workshops are also mobile.

Guerilla War to Revolutionary War

Last but not least among the movement's achievements is that as well as building a movement that remains ethnically open and with no religious bias, they achieved remarkable military success in 1977 and 1978. Indeed their miltary achievements are unique in Africa. The armed struggle has deep roots within the population. They have stuck to the countryside. Unlike most movements in Africa, there are no bases outside the country. There is a popular misconception that it was and is a guerilla war, whereas in fact it took the form of a revolutionary war.

The period 1975-77 could be correctly termed one of 'guerilla war'. But this had in fact come to a stop in 1977. Between 1977 and 1978 it was transformed into a 'revolutionary war'. That means the EPLF was on the offensive. It was no longer simply engaged in hit-and-run raids. This corresponds to the third phase of 'people's war', as classically outlined by Mao Tse-tung in China and Vo Nguyen Giap in Vietnam.* Very few movements have reached this offensive stage. The nearest to it, in Africa, was the PAIGC led by Amilcar Cabral in Guinea Bissau. But, successful as it was in wresting much of the countryside from Portuguese control, that movement was not able, due principally to demographic factors, actually to take the cities. In this respect the struggle led by the EPLF is unmatched in Africa, Latin America and Asia except for those of the Chinese and Indo-Chinese people.

The taking of Keren — let alone the other towns and cities — represented a great victory. Militarily, it probably compares favourably with the British campaign to drive out the Italians from the highlands of Eritrea and Ethiopia in the Second World War. By the end of 1977, the beginning of 1978, the EPLF forces reached the peak of their offensive. All major roads in the country were by then under the control of the EPLF, as were all the major cities of the Plateau and of the Highlands except Asmara, which was surrounded, and Massawa, which was under offensive siege. Most of the countryside, except the Dankalia and Barka Provinces, was under their control. These offensives were accompanied by the widespread mass mobilisations that we have referred to earlier.

The Present Stage

This position was, of course, dramatically changed as a result of the participation of the Soviet Union and Cuba on the side of Mengistu's

---

* These three phases are classically described as i) that of *strategic defence*, characterised by mobile warfare, a strategy of retreat to extend the aggressor's means of communication with some hit-and-run guerilla stikes, ii) one of preparation for a counter offensive where *guerilla warfare* becomes widespread, with strikes against the enemy's weak spots and mobilisation of the people, and iii) *revolutionary war*, that of the counter-offensive, when guerilla tactics merely support positional attacks against the enemy's strong points. (Editors)

regime in Ethiopia. Cuban training programmes and the provision of extremely heavy war materials, plus military aid from the Soviet Union have helped Mengistu to survive and recover. In October and November 1978 the overall balance of forces in Eritrea changed. The EPLF was driven back from the offensive, and from holding major towns and roads, back once again to guerilla warfare, which is logically now the way to fight.

'Can the EPLF in fact fight on?' everyone asks. They are going back to the mountainous areas and to classical guerilla warfare methods. Using these, they can survive as long as the Sudan is open to them logistically. The war could well go on then for years and years, until another change in the balance of forces. It is remarkable that they can still hold the city of Nakfa after so many months of Ethiopian siege.

Perspectives on the Eritrean Liberation Struggle

There is an inclination on the left and on the right to approach situations from a fixed ideological premise. The Eritrean situation is, however, extremely confusing. Yesterday when the world was apparently simple and straightforward, it was reassuring to see the United States backing Emperor Haile Selassie in Ethiopia, who was in turn fighting against a liberation movement backed by 'progressive' countries. Today we have the reverse pattern: a regime in Ethiopia claiming to be Marxist-Leninist suppressing liberation movements in Eritrea and the Ogaden, and behaving imperially.

Several levels and stages have in fact to be comprehended in coming to terms with this new situation. At one level, we must realise that Ethiopia extended its empire in the 19th century in the reign of Menelik II. As in Eritrea, the people of the Ogaden are opposed to continued Ethiopian domination.

At another, geo-political and geo-strategic level, the heart of the matter is control of the Red Sea. The USSR certainly entertains geopolitical and geo-strategic ambitions. They in turn claim that the Red Sea could become a Saudi Arabian and Arab 'lake', if the Eritrea Liberation Front (which is getting aid from these countries) rather than the EPLF, were in the forefront of an independent Eritrea. This is critical for the USSR once it shifted its support from Somalia to Ethiopia, which does not have an Arab 'connection'. Ethiopia itself wants, in turn, access to the sea which is only possible if it clings on to Eritrea. And indeed Ethiopia would be of little strategic significance to the USSR without a sea link. There is, in short, no ideological justification for the situation, but state interest, and geostrategies.

One principle, however, holds. Whatever changes of policy are made by states called 'Socialist', the right to self-determination, the right to be free remains. On this premise, we find the claims of the EPLF totally legitimate.

The Changing Situation in Eritrea

Dan Connell

In its eighteenth year Eritrea's tenacious struggle for national liberation is the longest – and by far the largest – armed conflict in the history of sub-Saharan Africa. It is amongst the most politically complex and least well-covered by the media. Its scale surpasses the much publicised war in the Ogaden which was front-page news in 1977.

Why is Eritrea given so little importance by the media and the world in general? The struggle there involves the Soviet Union in a major land war whose end is not in sight. Strategically, it is one of the most important areas – at the crossroads of Europe, Africa and Asia with the two key ports of Massawa and Assab on the Red Sea. One reason for the lack of interest may well be that in spite of the Soviet involvement the EPLF, unlike the Somali régime, have not turned elsewhere for backing.

The Eritreans have sustained serious military setbacks in recent months, leading many western commentators to join Soviet and Ethiopian propagandists in declaring the long and bitter war over. This is far from the case.

In the aftermath of Ethiopia's re-occupation of all the major towns previously held by the EPLF, the Eritreans have shifted their tactics from conventional seige and assault warfare to surprise guerilla-style actions against the now extended Ethiopian Government supply lines and numerous small garrisons. With the rapidly escalating Soviet presence in Eritrea on the side of Ethiopia's ruling military Dergue, the outlook now is for the war to continue without decision for the forseeable future, following a pattern roughly analogous to that of the Vietnam war in the late 1960s.

International Dimensions

If the Soviet Union's apparent willingness to commit itself to such an unenviable proposition should come as a shock, what is perhaps more surprising is that the Eritrean revolutionaries stoically and stubbornly refuse to react to it by running to the host of anti-Soviet forces who wish to help them. Instead they doggedly cling to their historical identification as an anti-imperialist movement and fight on without aid if necessary.

Five visits to Eritrea over the past three years, including a month-long tour of the EPLF-controlled areas that coincided with the latest round of fighting, lead me to conclude that Eritrean predictions of eventual if costly victory are justified. Such a victory would have far-reaching consequences — destabilising Soviet and American détente by undercutting their ability to control Third World movements and countries — and it is therefore viewed with apprehension by virtually all the world's major powers.

The United States and Arab countries in the region have long feared the emergence of an independent Marxist-orientated Eritrea. The domination of the divided Eritrea movement by the leftist EPLF has done little to lessen these fears. EPLF leaders have repeatedly insisted that there will be no political compromise with right-wing forces anxious to gain influence in Eritrea, and there is no sign that the EPLF's political line of national democratic revolution through protracted people's war is wavering.

At the same time, the EPLF's persistent refusal to compromise with either the Soviet Union or the Dergue on the question of Eritrea's right to full self-determination, as well as on other key political questions, has led many Eastern bloc countries to side against them in spite of earlier declarations of support. While the EPLF has loudly condemned Soviet actions in support of the Dergue in Eritrea, it has stopped short of blanket denunciation of 'social imperialism', which appears to have held China back from offering its support.

Thus isolated in the international arena, the Eritreans are forced to depend upon their own ingenuity and their internal resources to continue to prosecute the war. But this is nothing new. In fact, this is the EPLF's main strength.

Eritrea, which was previously an Italian colony, became a political football at the UN at the end of the Second World War, when Britain, France and the United States were anxious to keep it in the Western 'camp'. This move was opposed by the Eastern bloc and in particular the USSR. A statement made by USSR Ambassador Vishinsky in 1950 is worth remembering:

> The colonial system is going through an acute crisis. Accordingly, in considering the fate of Eritrea — one of the former Italian colonies — the UN must take a decision which will satisfy the longing of the Eritrean people for independence and freedom from national oppression. The General Assembly cannot tolerate a deal by the colonial powers at the expense of the population of Eritrea. In the circumstances, the only just solution . . . is to grant independence.

Over the first fifteen years of struggle, initially under the ELF, but later the EPLF and ELF, the guerilla movement severely disrupted Ethiopia's control over the territory and was met by an escalating US and Israeli-supported counter-insurgency strategy that included

Vietnam-style 'strategic hamlets' and indiscriminate rural bombing and urban repression in exchange for military bases in Eritrea.

Over the three years from 1974-1977, the Eritreans, mainly through the EPLF, gained control of the entire 42,000 square mile countryside and all but five towns and cities, while defeating three successive Ethiopian counter-offensives. In the aftermath of Vietnam, the US was reticent to get sucked into a bigger war, and by the middle of 1977 it looked as if an Eritrean victory was at hand.

The Soviet Role

Today, the tables have turned. The US and Israel are out of Ethiopia to the extent that military assistance has stopped, though there are still important economic ties. The EEC, the Soviet Union and Cuba are in. It is in effect a new war — a second war of national liberation.

Soviet combat personnel played a key role in the planning and battlefield execution of Ethiopia's latest seven-month military campaign in Eritrea, but it appears that Cuba held back from direct involvement. Two Soviet generals commanded the overall operation while lower echelon officers took charge of frontline units down to the battalion level. Between 150 and 250 Russian officers were deployed on every battlefront during the last weeks of fighting. The result was a dramatic change in tactical execution and a marked increase in the efficiency of the heavy weapons, which gave Ethiopia its first victories in Eritrea in years and substantially altered the character of the war.

Sophisticated intelligence gathering by Soviet-piloted helicopters and MIG jets, as well as satellite photographs, provided the Soviet planners with the means to organise the campaign. General Petrov, who ran the successful USSR-backed Ethiopian campaign against Somali forces in the Ogaden earlier this year, was the top commander of the Ethiopian ground forces in the Eritrean campaign, whilst another Soviet general commanded the Air Force.

Eleven Soviet officers of the rank of Lieutenant Colonel commanded the frontline units when the campaign against the EPLF opened on five simultaneous fronts in mid-November 1978, and lower officers commanded the smaller combat units. EPLF intelligence reports, based on intelligence sources inside the Ethiopian army and on intercepted radio communications, name Lt. Col. Alexei Alexandrov as the commander of the Ethiopian forces on the western front, Lt. Col. Vassily as the eastern front commander, and Lt. Col. Eduard as the northern front commander.

One of them, Lt. Col. Eduard, was fatally wounded in a battle at the town of Elaboret in late November, 1978, and died later in Addis Ababa. This was confirmed to me in Khartoum by US intelligence reports. Many frontline fighters also saw Russian corpses in and around Ethiopian tanks destroyed in the Elaboret fighting. One told me that

he examined a white body in a burned T54 tank who had in his pockets
a tube of Colgate toothpaste, three packets of Nyala cigarettes and
several small cakes.

The Military Character of the 'New' War

The new Soviet presence changed the character of the war by escalating
it to a higher level of sophistication through the introduction of massive
quantities of armoured vehicles, heavy artillery and air support which
was for the first time fully coordinated against the lightly armed
guerillas. In sharp contrast to earlier Ethiopian assaults characterised
by human wave attacks by the largely peasant militia and random aerial
and artillery bombardment, the current battles saw complex tactical
manoeuvres on multiple fronts, preceded by intensive pinpoint bombing and shelling on carefully selected weak points in the EPLF's de-
fences. The new Soviet-designed tactics centre around lightning drives
by self-contained armoured and infantry forces which more closely
resemble the Nazi 'blitzkrieg' than the human wave tactics of Stalinist
Russia and Ethiopia's previous Eritrean campaigns.

The latest Eritrean fighting started in mid-November, 1978, after a
two-month lull, following a series of unsuccessful Ethiopian attempts
to reach Keren. Hundreds of Soviet-supplied and in some cases Russian-
driven armoured cars and tanks spearheaded drives against EPLF
positions by more than 150,000 Ethiopian troops under Soviet command on five simultaneous fronts. Despite their numbers the infantry
appeared to play a secondary role to MIG fighter bombers, heavy
artillery and Stalin's organs (multiple rocket launchers) which pounded
away at long range at light-armed guerillas to open narrow paths for
concentrated thrusts by armoured vehicles.

Whilst Ethiopian radio was announcing spectacular victories, the
EPLF could be seen retreating a brigade at a time to the strategic,
rugged mountain areas around Keren where they took advantage of the
more favourable terrain to make a stand. Supplies of ammunition were
also convoyed into this area.

The situation changed when the Ethiopians mounted a surprise
flanking attack from the Red Sea coast. The EPLF had to drain its
rear garrisons to repel this attack which they did successfully. With
the new threat to their rear base area and crucial supply lines, the EPLF
was again forced to pull back and consolidate, yielding Keren, but not
before engaging the main Ethiopian forces there in one final, climactic
battle. I was not there, but listened to it. In numerous independent
interviews with the guerillas and EPLF commanders who participated
in the two-day battle of Elaboret, the following picture emerged.

Battle for Keren

At first light 90 Soviet T54 and BTR60 tanks clanked into the narrow valley along the asphalt road that bisects the lush citrus plantation until they stretched along its entire length.

Before the 35,000 man infantry force was over the lip of the vale the guerillas leapt from hidden positions among the bougainvillaea on both sides of the road to face the tanks in hand-to-hand combat using rocket-propelled grenades and homemade, Chinese-style, wooden-handled bombs. Taken by surprise, the tanks pivoted and spread out in disarray among the orange trees as the infantry flowed behind them. Some 25-30 tanks were abandoned at the forward end of the column, cut off from the others, but the EPLF was later forced to burn all but seven of them for lack of a way out.

For the next forty-eight hours the fighting raged up and down the surrounding hills with the Ethiopians almost breaking through to Keren early on day two, only to be pushed back again.

One fighter who came on the second day told me later:

'When we reached Elaboret it was full of tanks, dead bodies and trucks from edge to edge. All the dry grass was totally burned and rows of trees were down from the tanks. The planes never stopped coming. They were dropping different types of bombs including napalm and at times the valley was so filled with smoke that you couldn't even see.

'On the road behind us I counted 25 tanks and seven Russian trucks captured and about five more burned. We pursued them from all the hills into the valley and they were surrounded.

'We heard them on the radio saying that they had no way out and didn't know what to do. Then two helicopters landed with Russian officers, and soon they tried another counter-attack, but that movement was crushed and we pushed them back. Then the sun set and the battle was over.'

Under cover of darkness, the EPLF silently melted away to try again to narrow the fighting to two fronts instead of three - one on the north side of Keren and a second near the Red Sea coast. The following week, four-day battles were simultaneously fought with the EPLF victorious to end the campaign in another stalemate.

It must be emphasised that the Ethiopian offensive was only partially successful, though the invading forces took the large towns, they failed to reach the three smaller towns of Alfabet, Nakfa and Karora or to penetrate the EPLF's guerilla base area in this region. These are the objectives of the next phase of the offensive for which Ethiopia has been mobilising and which will get under way later in 1979.

More importantly, from the perspective of the war as a political struggle, the Dergue utterly failed to win popular Eritrean support in its military advance. The reoccupation of the large towns was preceded by a mass civilian exodus to the countryside, which remains almost entirely under guerilla control.

None of the towns was actually taken by military force. Instead, the EPLF fought outside the towns and pulled back after they were fully evacuated. The retreat of their large military units was carried out systematically to contract the fixed base area to a third the size it had been seven months ago.

Today the EPLF's fully liberated base is in the arid Sahel mountains, bordered on the east by the Red Sea and on the north by Sudan, while defended on the west and south by entrenched brigade-size units.

How strong is the EPLF today?

In the most recent three-week series of major battles, the EPLF captured more than 25 Soviet-supplied T54 tanks and BTR60 armoured cars to bring the number of armoured vehicles in their hands to more than 80. This is more then Ethiopia itself possessed under the US- and Israeli-backed régime of Haile Selassie only four years ago, and it gives the EPLF a better-equipped armed force than most established African states.

Guerilla losses on the battlefield appeared to be relatively high under a punishing bombardment by long-range Soviet-operated artillery, Stalin's organ rockets and MIG jet aircraft using napalm and cluster anti-personnel bombs, but the civilian evacuations also brought thousands of fresh volunteers that appeared sufficient to maintain the EPLF's infantry strength at 25,000 to 30,000 men and women.

Still, the EPLF clearly lacks the overall strength now to defeat the Ethiopian army in multiple, open-field confrontations. They lack sources of outside arms supply and have no effective defence against artillery, rockets and aircraft. Nor do they have enough ground forces to match those of Ethiopia.

As a result, the EPLF has begun a rapid transition to the mobile guerilla tactics that characterised the early years of the war, demobilising brigade-size units into companies and battalions, which are being deployed in loosely defined guerilla zones throughout the Eritrean countryside.

January, 1979

The Ethiopian 'Red Terror'

Mary Dines

Ethiopia's 'Red Terror', the system of control through fear and repression organised by the Dergue, has spread to the captured towns of Eritrea, where hundreds of people have been slaughtered. However, unlike the 'Red Terror' in Ethiopia, where in 1977 victims were butchered in the streets, the killings take place secretly.

The arrests and executions are organised by *kebeles* — district committees run on the same lines as those in Ethiopia.

When the Ethiopians re-occupied the main towns of Eritrea in November and December, 1978, they announced their intention of working through the mass organisations built up by the Eritrean People's Liberation Front (EPLF) by putting in leaders they could trust — often former servants of the Emperor Haile Selassie.

These newcomers were fiercely opposed, so the Ethiopians dismantled the former EPLF groups and set up *kebeles* as a means of social and political control.

In Asmara in particular the *kebeles* have played a leading role, especially in the arrest and execution of young people who are suspected of opposition to the Dergue or try to leave the city. Many hundreds have disappeared after being picked up in the streets. Relatives dare not ask questions about their whereabouts.

These activities, together with the behaviour of the Ethiopian troops, who assault and rape women and steal property and animals for food, have led to a mass exodus of the young from Asmara, especially of girls between the ages of 14 and 25. Most have managed to bribe or deceive the Ethiopian security guards and have slipped out into the countryside to join the EPLF.

News of the executions reaches the community only through other prisoners. Many of those arrested, like fifty young people arrested in Keren in May, are never heard of again.

There is a concentration camp for political detainees at Adi Quala, near Mendefera, which has become notorious for its brutality. Here, many prisoners have been strangled with wire, and in April three prisoners were paraded in front of the other inmates and battered to death with shovels.

The Dergue is now intensifying this new wave of 'Red Terror' with extortion, more arrests and killings, and the abduction of peasants to serve in the Ethiopian militia.

Many tricks are used by the authorities to extort money. In Keren, for instance, they recently announced that sugar, which is in very short supply there, would be on sale at 6 o' clock on a particular morning. Notwithstanding the fact that there is a curfew from 6.00 p.m. to 6.00 a.m., a large number of peasants crowded into the market area shortly before six in order to be certain of getting supplies. All were promptly arrested for being in breach of the curfew and were released only after they had been able to raise money to pay heavy fines.

Further south, in the highlands, peasants have traditionally farmed on land in the valley of the River Filfil, but are no longer able to go there as their crops have been burned and they themselves attacked by Ethiopian 'planes. They are, therefore, short of both food and money.

In April, the *kebele* in the local town of Zagar announced that there was to be a compulsory feast in aid of starving peasants in the Wollo province of Ethiopia. At this feast a number of items were put up for auction; all had to be sold. They included pieces of cloth stamped with slogans such as 'Ethiopia or death'. Anyone who refused to cooperate was arrested.

Fines have also been introduced for a large number of offences, including failure to turn up at *kebele* meetings. More recently, the Ethiopian authorities have started a practice of beginning arrests at 5.30 p.m. for 'breach' of the 6.00 p.m. curfew. They are not released until fines arc paid.

In January, 1979, a group of peasants grazing their cattle on the outskirts of the village of Merhano, near Asmara, were surrounded by armed *kebele* guards and fifteen people were carried away to serve in the Ethiopian militia. Their whereabouts are unknown.

The *kebele* also act as tax collectors. The Dergue has announced that everyone has to pay four years' back taxes and attempts to collect the money are now going on. In many cases, the sums involved are beyond the peasants' capacity to pay, but inability to do so is seen as 'counter-revolutionary'. Many, therefore, borrow from the few who have money.

The *kebele* have arrested many people for listening to the EPLF radio station — 'Voice of the Eritrean Masses' — which can be heard all over Eritrea and in the adjacent Ethiopian province of Tigrai. Arrests are particularly high in Tigrai, where the Dergue is trying to put down the peasant-based Tigrai People's Liberation Front with 30,000 troops, tanks, saturation bombing and mass arrests of the young, as in Eritrea. This conflict, about which the Dergue is desperately trying to suppress information, is now in its fourth year.

Eritreans have received none of the food aid given to Ethiopia. In Asmara last autumn food intended for the poor was distributed through the *kebeles* and much of it was side-tracked to friends and relatives of *kebele* leaders or on to the black market. Some has since been seen in Ethiopian army stores in Decemhare, which were captured by the

Eritreans in May.

Like the *kebele*, the Ethiopian army is feared in Eritrea for its violence and unpredictable behaviour. Many town dwellers have left for the countryside, gone as refugees to Sudan or joined the EPLF in the mountains.

Nomadic people are at particular risk from the Ethiopians. In Sahel province they and their animals are bombed if they are seen by the Ethiopian 'planes which fly daily over the area. If possible, the nomads move around at night. Like the town dwellers, some have gone to Sudan, and an increasing number are joining the EPLF.

The civilian population of Eritrea still plays a vital role in the guerilla war to evict the Ethiopians from their territory. The Ethiopian army's authority is limited to the towns they have occupied and garrisoned and they never venture into the countryside except in a convoy. They have a growing problem in getting supplies into towns outside Asmara because the roads are controlled by the EPLF, who still have many units fighting in the highlands and the south. The road from Massawa to Asmara, for instance, is still under Eritrean control.

Troop and convoy movements from the towns are reported by the civilians to EPLF units, who either mine or ambush convoys. In recent months, the Ethiopians have lost hundreds of trucks and other vehicles, thousands of tons of ammunition and other supplies and many troops as a result of EPLF activities.

(Reproduced from the 'Observer' Foreign News Service, July 4th 1979)

External Involvement in Ethiopia and Eritrea

Lars Bondestam

Introduction

In 1974-75 three seemingly unrelated events in Africa had a great impact on political developments in the continent: the Moroccan invasion of West Sahara, the civil war in Angola, and the proclamation of 'Ethiopian Socialism'. They were linked by the engagement of third parties: POLISARIO, MPLA and the Ethiopian military junta were supported by countries like Tanzania, Algeria, Libya, South Yemen, Soviet Union, East Europe and Cuba. On the other barricade one found Zaire, Mauretania, Morocco, Egypt, Sudan and Saudi Arabia, backed by western powers, particularly USA and France. The splits within OAU and the Arab League reflect the contradictions between the two camps.

The complicated conflicts in the Horn of Africa attracted increased international interest. The vacuum caused by a slow, uncertain and partial US withdrawal from Ethiopia was filled by the Soviet Union, Eastern Europe and Cuba.* Early in 1977, troops of the (right wing) Ethiopian Democratic Union (EDU) invaded western Gondar. The danger of the incursion was purposely exaggerated by both the Provisional Military Administrative Council (PMAC, or the 'Dergue') and by its new supporter, the Soviet Union, who described it 'an imperialist invasion'. Consequently, the Third Division of Harar was transferred to Gondar, whereby the Ogaden was left more or less open to the Somali army. When tanks and artillery were stuck in the mud around Metema and Humera in Gondar, Soviet arms and weapons were flown into Ethiopia on an ever-increasing scale. Thereby, the Soviet bloc landed in great trouble, standing with one foot in Somalia and one in Ethiopia. Subsequently, the Soviet Union and Cuba were expelled from Somalia and strengthened their grip on Ethiopia — Soviet military advisers in Mogadishu crossed the border to join the Dergue.

'Fighting a war against the imperialists on three fronts', as the Dergue saw it, they became entirely dependent upon Soviet military aid. Officially, the Soviet Union helped Ethiopia on ideological grounds, and they interpreted any opposition to the Dergue as political

---

* Moscow has made it a rule to offer arms assistance whenever the West refuses to do so — c.f., the support of Gowon in the Nigeria-Biafra civil war.

expressions of western imperialism and counter-revolution. From that Kremlin perspective the loss of Eritrea would be disastrous to the Ethiopian revolution and thereby to the Soviet presence in the Horn of Africa. These interests of Moscow have cost the Eritrean and the Ethiopian peoples tremendous human and material losses.

Advocates of the Soviet penetration of Ethiopian internal affairs point to the correct stand of Soviet Union and Cuba in their support of MPLA, whereas their intervention in the Horn is a manifestation of inconsistency in Soviet foreign policy. Another aspect of such inconsistency is the Soviet position on Western Sahara. Why doesn't the Soviet Union give full support to Polisario? Because of Soviet concern about Moroccan phosphates? Irrespective of a possible correlation of the interests of the Soviet Union and the Angolan people, in Ethiopia the contradiction is between the Soviet-supported Dergue and the Ethiopian peoples, the latter having more in common with the liberation of the African peoples than the Dergue will ever have. This requires some explanation.

The official line of socialism in Ethiopia is actually undermined by the Dergue itself. None of the characteristics of a socialist mode of production are fulfilled in Ethiopia, at least not within the centrally controllable sectors of the economy. The nationalisation of financial institutions and of the large industries only implied a transfer of ownership from private holders to the state. The labourers' control over production is as non-existent as ever. Surplus labour is at the command of the Dergue and the surplus value is used destructively against the people instead of being invested in a better life for the Ethiopians. The idea of democracy and of a free party has been suppressed by the Dergue's violent liquidation of left-wing parties, notably the Ethiopian People's Revolutionary Party (EPRP). The gap between the aims of the Ethiopian people's struggle of 1974 and the politics from above of today is as wide as that between socialism and military dictatorship. These are important facts which are crucial in understanding the difference between, for instance, Angola and Ethiopia, in exposing the rationale for Soviet support of the Dergue.

In order to better judge Ethiopia's new international dependence, I start with a brief review of American interests and strategy, which were in many respects different from the Soviet ones. With a longer experience of third world contacts and after the lessons of Vietnam, the US is more subtle in gaining profit than the Soviet Union. The advent of the harsh Soviet policy in Ethiopia is a new experience to the Ethiopians. This policy is discussed with particular reference to the new Soviet attitude to the Eritrean question. Also the new position of Cuba, which seems to follow her bigger ally, is considered. The oft-repeated question, whether Soviet and Cuban soldiers actually fight in Eritrea, is briefly surveyed, but here I want to stress that from an ideological point of view it makes no difference whether they take an

active part in the war with guns in their hands, or they 'only' serve
as arms suppliers, military advisers and mechanics, organisers of logistics,
etc.
The military presence of the eastern bloc in Ethiopia is interlinked
with its non-military activities there. The Dergue's rigid handling of
the Eritrean question (and of the question of nationalities in Ethiopia
in general) involves heavy sacrifices by both the Eritrean and the
Ethiopian peoples, as does the Soviet civil aid to Ethiopia. Thus,
Ethiopia's rapidly growing economic dependence on the Soviet bloc is
a direct function of her military dependence, which will continue so
long as the Dergue sticks to its policy of keeping the country together
with the help of guns, tanks, artillery and MIG-fighters. A section on
the co-operation between the Soviet bloc and Ethiopia is, therefore,
an essential part of this essay. Finally, I will try to show that the
Soviet Union will one day inevitably face the same fate as in Sudan,
Egypt and Somalia, i.e. the Ethiopian experiment with the Kremlin's
version of Marxism will not last too long.

US Imperialism in Ethiopia up to 1974

The US imperialist strategy of economic exploitation of Ethiopia's
human and material resources can be divided into a number of stages:
1. US military aid, which started in the early 1950s, aimed at security
within the country, by tying a growing Ethiopian military strength to
western ideology in order to 'keep communism at arm's length', to
quote a former US Assistant Secretary of State for African Affairs[1].
2. A semi-military programme, the Mapping Mission of the USAID,
started in the early 1960s. They produced maps of all Ethiopia from
aerial photographs, which gave the USA a useful knowledge of the topography and geography of the country.
3. The mapping was simultaneously supplemented with the collection
of information on the ground, the two main instrumental bodies being
the Malaria Eradication Service of the USAID and the Peace Corps.[2]
4. The security and accumulation of facts on all aspects of Ethiopian
life were necessary conditions for safe and profitable potential US
investments. Other conditions, like improved infrastructure (mainly
bridges and airports), more skilled Ethiopians (c.f. the US ideological
influence at the Haile Selassie I University and at the Alemaya Agricultural College), and a favourable government investment policy,
were fulfilled to some extent through USAID and the infiltration of
American personnel in key ministries, not least in the Planning Commission (where also at least one of the American advisers was directly
linked to the CIA). Various American finance institutions — banks and
insurance companies — were established.
5. There were also several important studies of investment opportunities, including pilot development schemes. US firms and institutes such
as the Stanford Research Institute, made investment reconnaissance

surveys to 'identify those projects, areas, commodities and markets which would *readily* be developed and which would yield the greatest revenue increases in the short-run'.

6. Eventually, preparations for important US investments started on a large scale in the early 1970s. An investment and export promotion centre was established with American capital. Several American firms showed their interest in investing in Ethiopia. Then came 1974.

Eritrea came into this picture in a number of ways. First, the risk of Arab, (i.e. anti-Israeli) expansion in the Red Sea area had to be checked. Second, a landlocked Ethiopia would hardly benefit US imperialist interests, and free access to the sea was of utmost importance. Third, the huge US investment in the Kagnew Communications Station required Ethiopian control in the area. Fourth, Eritrea, having reached a much more advanced capitalist stage than Ethiopia, with its infra-structure, industry and comparatively highly skilled manpower, would be a haven for American capital. These factors explain the USA's vote in favour of an Eritrean federation with Ethiopia at the UN in 1950, and her military and other support to the emperor's government against the Eritrean struggle for self-determination. The later Soviet interests in Ethiopia only overlap those of the USA to a limited extent. Moreover, the sophisticated US strategy was qualitatively different from the rather brusque entry of the next super-power on the Ethio-pian scene.

The Soviet Union and Eritrea

When the future of Eritrea was being debated at the UN in 1950 the Soviet delegate stated that the US favouring of a federation with Ethiopia reflected the interests of colonial powers led by the US:

> How is it possible to talk about a compromise if it has been adopted without the consent of the concerned people, i.e. without the parti-cipation of the Eritrean people? . . . Under these circumstances the most equitable solution to the problem of the future of Eritrea is to guarantee its independence.

Despite an increased national and political awareness among the Eritrean peoples and their growing repudiation of any form of political co-operation with Ethiopia, the Soviet standpoint has now changed in the opposite direction: 'Regional autonomy is the most progressive and acceptable form of self-determination'[3]. But this is not enough; the immense Soviet military support to Ethiopia's aggression in Eritrea points not only to regional autonomy but in fact to total annexation. The growing antagonistic contradictions between the labouring people of Eritrea and those of Ethiopia, artificially caused by this aggression, have nothing to do with the Leninist principles of national self-deter-mination, which the Kremlin claims to nurture. The aggravation of these contradictions stems from Soviet strategic interests in the Horn of Africa.

Concerning such interests, the Soviet Ministry of Foreign Affairs declared, on 3 February 1978:

The Horn of Africa is primarily of military, political and economic importance. The importance of the region is mainly because of its situation, where the two continents of Africa and Asia meet. There are many good harbours in the Persian Gulf and in the Indian Ocean. Moreover, there are maritime routes which link the oilproducing countries with America and Europe[4]

The Indian Ocean and its littoral states have attracted a military race in the area between West and East. The USA have a satellite tracking station on Mahe Island, a communications base at Diego Garcia, they have use of a Royal Air Force base at Masirah Island (Oman), and had the Kagnew Station in Asmara. The US military are involved in such states as Saudi Arabia, Kuwait and — not least — Iran[5]). The Soviet Union hopes to prevent the west from exercising unfettered influence in the area, which explains her ports in Aden and at the Island of Socotra (South Yemen), in Iraq and at Berbera (Somalia, closed in September 1977).

The power that controls the Red Sea will also control the valuable short cut between Europe and Asia. The Ethiopian leader, Lt. Col. Mengistu Haile Mariam, has warned that the 'USA is trying to establish a pact of reactionary states — Sudan, Egypt, and Saudi Arabia — in the region'. These threats may throw some light on the 'Soviet (balancing) presence in the area and its interests in Ethiopia and Eritrea. As one commentator has put it:

The potential of this alliance could be formidable, as it would comprise about two-thirds of the total land area of the Arab world, half its population and 40% of its proven oil reserves. More importantly, however, the apparently increasing US military and economic efforts in the Sudan, Egypt and Saudi Arabia could help these countries establish their hegemony on the Red Sea[6].

In 1972, the Egyptian newspaper *Al Ahram* renamed the Red Sea the Arab Sea, 'as all states dominating it are Arab'. This naturally stirred up antagonistic feelings in Ethiopia, which was omitted from the list of the littoral states. Since then the USA has replaced the USSR in two of the most important Red Sea states, Sudan and Egypt, and apart from South Yemen, the only Russian contact with the Red Sea is Eritrea.

This means that Eritrea has become a meeting ground of Soviet and Ethiopian interests. It is in the Soviet interest to favour a government which seeks military solutions to the various conflicts, whereby Ethiopia will remain dependent on a continuous supply of Soviet weapons and military technology. Ethiopia also offers an excellent testing ground of Soviet arms and military tactics. Hence the active Soviet support in favour of Mengistu in late 1976 and early 1977 when Teferi Bante, who represented a softer line toward Eritrea, threatened his position. The ambassadors of the Soviet Union, East Germany and Cuba were the first to congratulate Mengistu on the successful execution of Teferi and the group around him in February 1977. Soviet actions here are similar to the much criticised US engagement in the internal affairs of other countries. All that has happened is a reversal of roles.

Cuba and Eritrea

Three lines could be noticed in Cuban politics after 1970: a pragmatic line, favouring the best possible alliances to improve the internal economy; the revolutionary line of Fidel Castro in supporting anti-imperialism in selected countries; and a military line, represented by Raúl Castro's push for military assistance to 'export the Cuban revolution'. The Cuban army was, during the 1960s, heavily engaged in civil activities, but with the strengthening of the civil administration, the army has now been released from these duties, which has reinforced the position of Raúl Castro. The success in Angola, which was Cuba's so far most ambitious engagement abroad, has further strengthened the line of the brothers, Fidel and Raúl Castro, at the expense of the so called pragmatists.

This, however, only partially explains the material *potentiality* of Cuban international engagement, but not how it is financed, not its ideology, and not why Cuba *actually* involved itself on the Ethiopian side. I shall not pretend to give answers to these questions but will make a few remarks.

Che Guevara's criticism (at the Afro-Asian Economic Seminar in Algiers in 1964) of the socialist countries, who 'exploit the under-developed ones through unequal exchange no less than the developed capitalist ones do', was never repeated after 1967. A change in Cuban foreign policy has actually been noticeable after the death of Che Guevara — from support of revolutionary opposition movements to support to progressive, already established, governments. This may explain to some extent the transfer of favour from the liberation front in Eritrea during Haile Selassie's time to the military junta in Addis Araba after 1975. But this drastic shift is nowhere justified in political terms[7]. The Cuban presence in Ethiopia was probably not initially decided in Havana, but was rather conditioned by the wishes of the Soviet Union.

Her dependence upon the Soviet Union means that Cuba has to adjust her foreign policy to that of her bigger brother. The co-operation between the two is illustrated in Africa, where, out of eleven countries, where Russian civil or military personnel are present, we find Cuba in ten of them. This is not sheer coincidence. Soviet and Cuban military personnel are co-operating in Ethiopia, if not entirely on the ideological level at least militarily against the Dergue's enemies. Shortly after the Soviet Union had established itself in Ethiopia, Fidel Castro indicated

negative views on the Eritrean liberation movements in an interview in
Afrique-Asie (16 May 1977). Since 1968, when Fidel Castro called the
Eritrean struggle a 'progressive revolution', the EPLF has emerged as
a more radical movement than the ELF, but Castro now calls them 'the
secessionists in the northern part of the country, who also at present
get assistance from the reactionary countries in the region'[8], and
similarly, 'yankee imperialism seeks to question Ethiopia's right to
defend its territorial integrity and unity against the Eritrean secessionists'[9]. Is Castro honest to his own ideology when he indicates
that both the character of EPLF and ELF and the 'territorial integrity
and unity' of Ethiopia depend on the character of the self-appointed
government in Addis Ababa?

However, the possibility of Cuba being in Ethiopia on behalf of the
Soviet Union does not necessarily imply a total Cuban acceptance of
Soviet and Dergue policy. A conceivable contradiction in the Cuban
and the Ethiopian views came into view in May 1978, when both the
Cuban and the South Yemen ambassadors to Ethiopia temporarily left
Addis Ababa. They had assisted Negede Gobezie's return from his
exile in Paris (where he had stayed since the Dergue-Meison split in
August 1977) to Addis Ababa, in order to build up a communist party
and to contribute to a political solution in Eritrea.*

To Fight or to Advise How to Fight?

The Soviet military aid to Ethiopia started in early 1977 and consists
of five components: arms supply, military advice, maintenance, training
and front line combat. Each one of these components is necessary to
conduct a war. Each one is useless without the others. Thus, active
participation in any of them also implies active participation in the
wars against the various Ethiopian and Eritrea peoples.

When the USA partly withdrew from Ethiopia in February 1977,
after the execution of Teferi Bante (due to violation of 'human rights'
according to the US Secretary of State, Cyrus Vance), she was immediately replaced by Soviet Union. The first consignment of Soviet
arms contained hundreds of thousands of light weapons: Kalashnikov
automatic rifles, machine guns, anti-tank rockets and grenade launchers.
They were used by the hastily trained peasant militia, first against the
Western Somalia liberation front (WSLF) and EDU and later in Eritrea.

In March 1977 the Soviet Union promised to supply the Dergue
with MIG-fighters, modern tanks, robot bombs and long-range artillery,
all valued about US$ 400 million. Ethiopia had foreign reserves of at
least US$ 300 million and was further backed by Libya and could
afford to shop around for arms. The next month the Dergue closed
down the US Information Service, the naval research unit, the Kagnew
Station, and the Military Assistance Advisory Group (MAAG). The

* 'MEISON' stands for the Amharic version of all Ethiopian Socialist Movement.
  Negede was one of its top leaders.

alliance between Ethiopia and the USA collapsed, whereby Ethiopia missed some US$ 100 million worth of previously approved arms supplies. The next month Mengistu travelled to Moscow to confirm the Soviet military assistance. In 1978 the Soviet Union and East Germany supplied Ethiopia with arms worth over US$ one billion.

As a consequence of the massive arms supply, Soviet, East German and Cuban personnel were the masters of military technology in Ethiopia, and they naturally took care of military strategy in the Ogaden. A special defence committee was established in the Ministry of Defence in Addis Ababa, consisting of Soviet, Cuban and Ethiopian officers. The committee stayed in office after the retreat of the Somali army, and is now directing the war in Eritrea (possibly without Cuban participation). Foreign military advisers have also been stationed in the war-zones, in Harar and Asmara respectively.

The maintenance and handling of the new arms demanded a large contingent of foreign experts — from the Soviet Union but mainly from 'third countries', Cuba and South Yemen. This implied active participation also at the war-fronts. Certain places, like the Debre Zeit air base and Siga Meda (militia camp west of the capital), were crowded with Russians and Cubans, in charge of the repair of arms and of the training of regular soldiers and of the peasant militia. Ethiopian military personnel were also trained in the Soviet Union, including some forty pilots who went there to learn to fly MIG-fighters.

In early August 1977 Somalia claimed that 5,000-9,000 foreign troops 'from a non-African country' (probably Cuba) had been sent to Ethiopia to fight the resistance in the south-east and in the north. This allegation was never confirmed, but later the Cuban Granma admitted active Cuban participation in the Ogaden war from January 1978 onwards. The next month it was rumoured that there were 5,000 Cuban soldiers in Ethiopia, a figure which US intelligence later increased to about 17,000, although American sources are hardly the most reliable when it comes to anti-American military engagement.

Up to mid-1978 the ELF had not officially admitted Soviet or Cuban presence in Eritrea (except that ELF asserted that Soviet pilots had taken part in the Ethiopian offensive at Massawa in December 1977), but Michael Duffy (AP reporter) had this to say after a visit to the area in May 1978:

> The question of the Cuban-Soviet presence is hot for the ELF, who were dependent on aid from the Soviet bloc in the mid-60s. In our contacts with 'grass-roots' of the ELF at the front we daily heard about hundreds of Cubans killed and many more taken prisoner after fights near Asmara. The Cubans were said to man tanks, artillery and other sophisticated material, supplied by the Soviet Union. But the higher up in the ELF hierarchy we came, the more reluctant people were to talk about the Cuban-Soviet presence . . . The General Secretary of ELF, Tesfai Wolde Michael, told us that there is

no proof of Cubans being active in the fighting and that ELF still regard them as their 'strategic friends[10].

ELF, on the other hand, have been more outspoken:

. . . the Ethiopian aggressor troops beseiged in Asmara launched a large-scale offensive from Asmara on 14 March 1978. The Ethiopian force was composed of 10 thousand-strong accompanied by 20 tanks and heavy air cover and heavy artillery. The Cuban-Ethiopian troops moved in a front 36 kms. wide . . . In their vain attempt to prolong the colonisation of Eritrea, the Ethiopian aggressors are flying in huge quantities of arms and troops to Asmara. The latest Cuban arrivals in the last two weeks alone have reached 1,500 bringing the total number of Cuban troops in Asmara along to 3,500[11].

The BBC had a reporter in Massawa in January 1978, who confirmed accusations that the Soviet Navy bombarded the port. Also other independent sources have mentioned the presence of foreign combat troops in Eritrea. Although Mengistu cannot be said to be particularly reliable, it is worth mentioning that he in a speech of gratitude in Harar on 16 May 1978 said of the Cubans they they are 'living with us, dying with us and fighting with us', and talked about 'blood being shed every hour on the battlefield', referring to soldiers from the Eastern bloc, who assisted the Ethiopian troops in Eritrea. But both Cuba and South Yemen were obviously troubled by their new role in Eritrea. They hesitated to send any of their troops to the northern front, and in June 1978 Cuba seems to have refused to give any military support to the offensive in Eritrea, which had just started.[12] But, and this cannot be repeated too often, so long as Cuban troops remain in Ethiopia and provide for the survival of the Dergue and for the release of Ethiopian military personnel from other fronts (particularly the Ogaden), Cuba also sustains the war in Eritrea.

The Soviet bloc was not the only arms supplier to Ethiopia. In February 1978 government sources in Washington revealed that Israel had furnished the Ethiopian regime with robot and napalm bombs (which may explain the rumoured visit by Mengistu and Michael Imru to Israel in July 1977). Shortly afterwards the Israeli foreign minister, Moshe Dayan, confirmed his country's military assistance to Ethiopia. An opposition politician in the Knesset and an important member of the Israeli foreign and defence committee, Yossi Sarid, then demanded the resignation of Dayan, as he 'had caused irreparable damage to Israel's security'. To save its face, the Dergue had to expel the Israelis from Ethiopia.

The Politics of Soviet-Third World Co-operation

There are superficial similarities between the Soviet Union of 1917 and Ethiopia of 1974. In February 1917 the aristocratic class was overthrown by the bourgeoisie, followed in October by a shifting of the balance of power in favour of the proletariat. Similarly, in Ethiopia, the more than ten year old class struggle between the aristocracy and the relatively modern national bourgeoisie was finally won by the latter, represented by Endelkachew Mekonnen. (The emperor wasn't formally overthrown until September, but in practice he lost power with the downfall of his government in February.) The struggle of the Ethiopian working class went on during the whole of 1974, and late that year they gained power with the proclamation of 'Ethiopian Socialism' — according to the Dergue version. At least we can agree that both revolutions 'created a situation in which the chances for emancipation of the urban working class were much improved, although subsequent developments were far from taking a rectilinear course'.[13]

The Dergue doesn't seek support only among the urban proletariat but also among the peasants of central and southern Ethiopia. In Soviet Marxist theory, however, the peasant component in a social revolution makes it basically petit bourgeois in character, and consequently it may deviate from its socialist course. We might here perceive a Soviet concern in guiding the Ethiopian revolution in the 'right direction', but this concern is of a pragmatic rather than of an ideological nature (ideological arguments are usually added later). It is also symptomatic that whereas Chinese aid to Ethiopia mainly goes towards small-scale improvements in the countryside (agriculture and health), the civil part of Soviet co-operation with Ethiopia is entirely within industry and commercial agriculture.

The Soviet Union was and is a multinational state, just as Ethiopia is. In Ethiopia there is an echo of Stalin's particular interpretation of Leninism and his 'solution' to the national question. The Red Army intervened within territories that were claimed as belonging to the Soviet orbit, e.g. when it went into Georgia in the early 1920s on Stalin's orders, an act not appreciated by either Lenin or Trotsky. There is no Lenin in Ethiopia today (although some seem to pretend there is), only a good portion of Soviet orthodox ideology (of the 1920s as well as of 1956, 1968, . . .) and a pragmatic Dergue. The Red Army was always said to intervene on the principle of supporting communist insurrections that had already arisen. In Ethiopia, on the other hand, after all condemnation of the Eritrean peoples, manifested in both propaganda and bombs, the intervention by the Dergue army is more difficult to justify from a revolutionary perspective — the component of class struggle is indeed fragile in a war conducted with tanks and artillery and from the air. After 1917 the Soviet leaders agreed that their revolution was not for export. Also today, when we critically scrutinise the sudden friendship between the Soviet and the Ethiopian regimes, we have to question 'the revolutionary motive' of Soviet assistance.

Since the mid-1950s the Soviet Union has supported revolutions in a number of countries, whose governments, however, did not always appreciate the eastern goodwill. However, after the events in the Congo 1961 (the fall of Lumumba), Iraq 1963 (Kassam), Algeria 1965 (Ben Bella), Indonesia 1965 (Sukarno), Ghana 1966 (Nkrumah) and Mali 1968 (Keita), Soviet leaders lost much of their previous optimism (and after Czechoslovakia 1968 would-be supporters of Soviet Union lost theirs). In Moscow, the term 'revolutionary democracies' was abandoned and 'the non-capitalist road to development', one much longer than Khruschev had dreamt of, introduced. Moreover, the Soviet Union didn't have sufficient resources to assist all those countries which claimed to be anti-imperialist, and Soviet bilateral contact became more selective. Among those singled out were also countries of significance for Soviet strategic interests and security policy.

The basic principles of Soviet aid to underdeveloped countries have not changed in the last two decades, but priorities have. Whereas political aspects were officially stressed up to the mid-60s, practical economic considerations have since then taken over more and more. Thus, Soviet support to liberate countries from imperialist domination has definitely not disappeared (cf. the support to Angola, Mozambique and liberation movements in Southern Africa), but the sheer economic gains that both receiver and donor can make out of respective bilateral co-operation is now particularly stressed.

Just as before the fall of Khruschev in 1964, the USSR still shows a great trust in the state sector of the underdeveloped countries, which is strengthened by nationalisation of foreign and domestic private property, industrialisation and expansion of economic ties with the eastern bloc. Consequently, the 'east-south' trade has increased rapidly during the past two decades, though is still small compared to the 'west-south' trade, and Soviet aid goes mainly to those countries where industry is state-owned.

The Soviet leaders are rather explicit in their formulation of the aims of Soviet co-operation with the third world[14]:
– to promote economic growth in the receiving country.
– to contribute to the production and export to Soviet Union of such commodities which are cheaper to produce or are in relative abundance in the underdeveloped countries.
– to promote a long economic co-operation and a planned 'socialist division of labour' between the Soviet bloc and the underdeveloped countries.

Thus, the law of comparative advantage is the ideological foundation of Soviet-Third World co-operation or, as Prime Minister Alexi Kosygin put it: 'The importance of a stable division of labour between Socialist and developing countries must be stressed'. When examining this co-operation we must agree with the Soviet leaders that 'trade, not aid' has become their guiding principle. But we may doubt whether this division of labour will at all benefit the weaker partners. Andre Gunder Frank has written:

. . . in regard to the factor proportions and the commodity composition of east-west and east-south trade, the underdeveloped countries are to the socialist ones as these are to the developed capitalist ones (or vice versa). In other words, the socialist countries occupy an intermediate position — in this regard not unlike the most developed 'sub-imperialist' underdeveloped countries, like Brazil — in the international division of labour; they import advanced technology manufactures from the industrially developed capitalist countries, paying for them with raw materials and incurring a growing trade deficit; and they export less sophisticated manufactures to the underdeveloped countries, with whom they run up a trade surplus, part of which they use to reduce their trade deficit with the imperialist countries — also not unlike the sub-imperialist capitalist countries.[15]

The guiding principle in price-fixing between the Soviet Union and the Third World is the ruling world market price for each commodity. Thus, the gains of trade are unequally distributed between them,

. . . for, the latter group of countries receive for their own wares prices which are barely higher than what they get from the West, while the USSR is able to extract considerably higher prices from the Third World than what it has been able to obtain from the West.[16]

Moreover,

. . . the Soviet Union maintains an artificially high value of the rouble, not in relation to convertible currencies, but as against inconvertible Third World currencies[17].

Andre Gunder Frank's analysis strikes at the heart of the Soviet model of 'socialism and proletarian internationalism:'

What experience does show is that the socialist countries of eastern Europe stick to business and drive as hard a bargain in international trade as anybody else . . . Within the capitalist underdeveloped countries, east-south economic relations do not significantly further the interests of the exploited producing classes — as distinct from the owning ones — any more than do capitalist west-south relations.[18]

From what has been said here it should be clear that the Soviet Union occupies a position in the world economy qualitatively different from that of the advanced capitalist countries. It is questionable whether any of Lenin's five basic features of imperialism can be applied to 'east-south' relations (creation of monopolies, creation of finance capital, export of capital, formation of international monopolist capitalist associations, and territorial division of the whole world among the biggest capitalist powers). Imperialism is just one form of exploitation of the underdeveloped countries. The forces of monopoly capital in the West do not exist in the planned economy of the East, nor do the effects, manifested in superaccumulation of capital. Thus, the Soviet Union is not looking for other markets to get rid of surplus production or surplus capital, but is rather aiming at covering the internal demand of certain commodities. The exports are a means to make the imports of such commodities possible. When placed aginst the history of imperialism as a stage of capitalist expansion, the inadequacy of the phrase 'social imperialism' seems clear.

The Ethiopian Experience of Co-operation with the Soviet Bloc

The Soviet Union supported already in 1976 the Ethiopian 'National Democratic Revolution Programme' and delegations came to pay homage to its designers. Various cultural agreements were signed and scholarships were offered to Ethiopian students (400 to the Soviet Union and 300 to East Europe, but the expenses of most of these students are covered by the Ethiopian government; some students in Moscow, who had questioned the Dergue, were sent back to Addis Ababa to be punished). A trade agreement was signed with East Germany and an agreement of co-operation with Czechoslovakia. When Mengistu made a state visit to the USSR in May 1977 a heap of bilateral agreements on trade and co-operation were drawn up. More agreements have been added since then.

In October 1977 an Ethiopian delegation went to East Germany to negotiate the terms of co-operation between the two countries. Where conflict arose between East German and Ethiopian interests, the host had the upper hand and directed the conditions. The Ethiopians were divided into two groups: one favouring Ethiopian interests even if that would lead to an East German refusal and a possible collapse of the negotiations, and another obedient to the tough East German terms and conditions and espousing socialist botherhood at any cost to the Ethiopian economy. Needless to say, the latter group came off winner. A deterioration of the already weak Ethiopian economy may eventually turn out to be the price of this Ethiopian dependence.

We know that the Soviet Union and East Europe buy cheap primary goods from underdeveloped countries and sell the same or the same kind of goods to other countries at higher prices. In exchange for imported arms and military technology from East Germany, Ethiopia is bound to sell most of its important export crop, coffee, for the next ten years, at a fixed price. After processing in East Germany, the coffee will be reexported to West Germany and elsewhere.

The Soviet Union and Ethiopia have signed several contracts of bilateral assistance, stipulating the conditions of aid given by the former to various Ethiopian state companies and authorities. They all look more or less the same. One of them was signed in late 1977 between a certain Ethiopian State Company (referred to below as ESC) and Vsesojuznoje Exportno-Importnoe Objedinenije 'Seklhozpromexport',

Ovchinnikovskaja nab., Moscow 113324 (hereinafter simply called VEI). According to this contract:

- VEI shall render technical assistance in the running of a number of plants.
- ESC shall pay the salaries of the VEI-experts, 750-1000 roubles per person a month (about US$ 1400-1800) for two years, and all taxes that may be levied upon the experts and upon one interpreter (the latter's salary paid by the Soviet government).
- ESC shall pay all air travel expenses of the experts and of their families, Moscow-Addis Ababa and back, plus extra luggage transport.
- ESC shall pay 36 days leave and up to two months of sick leave per year plus extra travel to Moscow and back (same conditions as above).
- ESC shall pay insurance expenses of the VEI-experts with the Soviet insurance company, Gosstrakh.
- ESC shall supply the VEI-experts and the interpreter with fully equipped offices and transport facilities and with fully furnished villas or first class hotel, with all modern conveniences, including refrigerators and air-conditioners both at the place of permanent work and during business trips.
- ESC shall supply the VEI-experts and the interpreter and their families with free medicine, medical aid and hospitalisation.
- ESC shall pay all travels of experts, interpreter and their families between Addis Ababa and the place of work – by plane, car or first class train.
- All payments shall be affected by ESC in roubles, via the Bank of Foreign Trade of the USSR.

The cost of this venture is conservatively estimated at about half a million US dollars. The salaries are paid to the Soviet government, and a portion of them goes back to VEI-experts. In practice, this means that the Soviet government, as an aid broker, makes a net profit out of the sale of Soviet know-how to Ethiopia. But it has turned out to be a high price for ESC – when the VEI-experts arrived it was found that they did not speak sufficient English (hence the interpreter who is supposed to serve simultaneously a dozen of his compatriots); they were technically unqualified for the jobs (partly due to the American or West European machinery); and they had no knowledge of the environment of the plants and of the actual conditions and processes of production.

Conclusion

During the American era in Ethiopia the majority of the population suffered immensely and many succumbed as a result of their economic exploitation. The various famines, ignored by the American-supported imperial government, costs hundreds of thousands of human lives – on top of an extremely high 'natural' death rate. Today, the poor peasants in southern and central Ethiopia have, in general, improved their material standards. But deaths due to famine have not disappeared* and hundreds of thousands of political victims have been added to the mortality statistics. These victims can be divided into three categories: enemies of the Dergue, active participants in the Dergue's revolution (willingly or unwillingly), and the inactive third part.

The first category consists of fighters and supporters of various national liberation movements, particularly in Ogaden, Eritrea, Gondar and Tigrai, and of members and supporters of active opposition groups, particularly EPRP. Air raids, bomb-attacks, indiscriminate massacres, mass killings, eradication of villages, communities and political prisoners — in brief this is the so called red terror. These immense Dergue offensives against its enemies would not have been possible without Soviet military support.

The second category consists of those soldiers and peasants who are forced or lured to fight in areas they have never been to, against people they never heard of, and in the name of a cause they never understood. The mobilisation of some two hundred thousand such people, of whom many are dead or crippled, again would not have been possible without external moral support and training and without large supplies of Soviet weapons with which they were furnished.

The mobilisation of human and capital resources for military purposes has negatively affected the third element, i.e. those people who are not actively engaged on any side of the armed conflicts. One example is the consequences for agricultural production when agricultural labour is recruited for the militia. Another example is the starvation in 1978 which could have been prevented at an earlier stage — if the means had been available. Despite the fact that this famine was predicted and that the Dergue was aware of it, already in late 1977 most resources — even some of the Relief and Rehabilitation Commission (RRC) vehicles — were expropriated to be used against the 'enemies of the revolution'[19]. Today, resources are mobilised by RRC to rescue the starving people, but unnecessary suffering could have been avoided, and at a much lower cost, a year earlier. These by-products of the military operations have not been considered as part of the 'comparative advantage' in the agreements on Soviet-Ethiopian co-operation.

After the USA met with a rebuff in April 1977 they abstained from voting when the question of two loans to Ethiopia was raised in the World Bank. But the lack of human rights and strong presence of the East in Ethiopia have not prevented imperialist powers from securing a foothold in the country: World Bank-loans of some US$ 100 millions were decided upon; in 1976 the EEC signed assistance for the period 1976-80 worth US$ 150 millions. During 1977/78 aid was given by West Germany, Sweden and engagement in Ethiopian affairs has defi-

* According to 1979 reports of the International Committee of the Red Cross, 1,800,000 people once again face famine in the Wollo and Tigre Provinces alone. (eds.)

nitely not disappeared. In a semi-secret circular from the Dergue early in August 1977 it was prohibited from that day on to write 'US imperialism' and 'Zionism' in any paper. The red colour of the Dergue's anti-imperialist label is fading.

One super-power cannot be judged on the basis of the policies of another, but few comparisons of the USA and Soviet Union will be made. Western aid to Ethiopia covered a broader field, including food and emergency assistance, than does Soviet and East European aid. At least up to December 1977, the only external aid of a humanitarian nature originated from the USA and West Europe. Most of the urban people have come into close contact with the political executions (friends and relatives), and prefer Carter's 'human rights' — whatever they are worth — to Bhreznev's weapons.

The American lecturers at the University have been replaced by Russians. American individualism has been replaced by Soviet Marxism (whose economic theories do not differ too much from those of American capitalism, previously taught). Open discussions during lectures are now prohibited. Most Soviet teachers don't speak understandable English and none of them accept contact with the students after lecture-hours. The American lecturers were never particularly appreciated by the students, but their successors are no more popular.

The new foreign experts isolate themselves from Ethiopian life more than westerners ever did. The language barriers also serve as barriers of understanding between the Ethiopians and the foreigners, particularly the Russians. The latters' information on daily political developments is limited to a minimum. This probably holds to some extent for the eastern embassies and intelligence departments as well, their only sources of information being the official Dergue propaganda and individual Ethiopian officers. Whereas the Cubans in Angola have direct communication with the ordinary inhabitants (Spanish-Portuguese), the Cubans in Ethiopia face great difficulties, not only in trying to understand the development and the true character of the military junta, but also in their capacity as civil servants — most of the civilian Cubans work in the field of medicine. (However, as the Cubans gradually learn English, the barriers between them and the Ethiopians will probably disappear, which in the long run may also change Cuban attitudes towards the Dergue and its enemies). The rigid social life of the foreigners, their position as aliens and their isolation are frustrating to them and may explain a number of strange incidents in which some of them have been involved (sometimes containing a dose of racialism), strongly disapproved by the Ethiopian public.

The eastern military support to the unpopular Dergue , the unfavourable conditions of co-operation between the Soviet bloc and Ethiopia, the alienation of the new foreigners from Ethiopian social life — these are factors which have fortified the barriers between particularly the Soviets and the Ethiopian bureaucratic and petty bourgeoisies and working classes. Social alienation has political implications spilling over into Ethiopian military circles.

If Mengistu is proven right when he said that 'The Eritrea war may continue for generations', the Ethiopians may have to live under Soviet hegemony for quite some time. But if Eritrea's right to self-determination is recognised and if it becomes a reality the Soviet Union will be evicted from Ethiopia, as their civil mission has no support among any social class in the country. The vicious circle of mutal dependence between the Dergue and the Soviet Union can be broken by overthrowing the former. A united and extended Eritrean struggle would be a crucial part of that process, as it was in the overthrow of Haile Selassie's regime in 1974.

References

1. Mennen Williams, *United States Policy in Africa*, (Special Report, Williams College), March 18, 1965, p.4.
2. For curiosity, here follows a sample of US organisations in Ethiopia in 1971: AFL-CIO, Aid for International Medicine, American Leprosy Missions, the American Lutheran Church, Christian Brothers, Church World Service, Eastern Mennonite Board of Missions and Charities, The Ford Foundation, Lutheran World Relief, Medical Missionaries of Mary. Medical Mission Sisters, Missionary Aviation Fellowship, The Orthodox Presbyterian Church, The Pathfinder Fund, Public Administration Service, Public Welfare Foundation, Rockefeller Foundation, Sudan Interior Mission, United Church Board for World Ministries, United Presbyterian Church in the USA, USAID, US Information Service, World Neighbours.
3. *New Times*, no.32, 1977.
4. *Keesings*, p.28992.
5. With the recent change in Iran, the US military presence there will cease, at least temporarily.
6. Madan Sauidie, in *Africa*, no.68, April 1977, p.53.
7. For one Cuban statement based on a misunderstanding of the Ethiopia of today and of her self-appointed head, Mengistu, see Raúl Valdés Vivó, *Ethiopia, the Unknown Revolution*, (Ciudad de la Habana, 1978).
8. Speech by Fidel Castro, 14 March 1978, translated from a quotation in Swedish in *Nyheter fran Kuba*, no.5, 1978, published by the Cuban Embassy in Stockholm.
9. Speech by Fidel Castro, quoted in *Granma*, 7 May 1978.
10. *Dagens Nyheter*, 13 May 1978, translated from Swedish.
11. *EPLF Military Communique*, 17 March 1978.
12. *Observer*, 11 June 1978.
13. W.F. Wertheim, *Evolution and Revolution*, (Penguin, 1974), p.165.
14. K. Eklund, *Sovjetunionen och u-länderna*, SIDA, Stockholm, May 1977, p.32.
15. Andre Gunder Frank, 'Long Live Trans-ideological Enterprise, Socialist Economies in Capitalist International Division of Labour', *Economic and Political Weekly*, (India) vol.12, no.6-8, p.305.
16. N.K. Chandra, 'USSR and Third World: Unequal Distribution of Gains', *ibid*, p.367.
17. *ibid*, p.373.
18. Gunder Frank, *op.cit.*; pp. 319 and 325.
19. L. Bondestam, *Expected Famine in Ethiopia*, (RRC, Addis Ababa, October 1977), where I showed that 'there is an inevitable risk of a famine in Ethiopia, possibly of the same magnitude as the one of 1973'.

PART III
THE SOCIAL REVOLUTION

The Social Revolution in Eritrea

Francois Houtart

Introduction

It is important to spell out the social dimensions of the Eritrean revolution because the people's participation and the profound structural transformation of society undertaken in the liberated zones under the control of the EPLF have been a crucial featue of this liberation struggle.

This strategy of liberation has ushered in political and socio-economic phenomena that are new in Africa's modern history. The EPLF's political line in this respect — which has definitely become the dominant character of the Eritrean liberation struggle as a whole — and the experiences acquired in its application in the seventies together with those of the victorious liberation movements of the ex-Portuguese colonies and the continuous struggle in Southern Africa (Namibia, Zimbabwe, South-Africa) constitute a precious patrimony in the continent's march towards its national and social liberation.

In order to have a deeper insight into the social revolution that is taking place in the Eritrean society, we deem it necessary to start in section I with the social analysis of pre-revolutionary Eritrea. In section II, we will examine the consequences of the liberation struggle on the social structure and on the relations of production in Eritrean society. The great bulk of this paper will be based on the policies and practices of the EPLF. However, we will point to the experiences and policies of the other Front and will make an overall analysis of the Eritrean Fronts and their political and social projects in our conclusion.

I ERITREAN SOCIETY BEFORE THE BEGINNING OF THE LIBERATION STRUGGLE

Eritrean society has been shaped both by its internal history and by external interventions. It has undergone different types of colonialism. Almost a century after the advent of the first modern European colonialism in the region, the Italian one, Eritrean society is today made up of various social classes, the great majority of the population being composed of peasants engaged in subsistence production in the context of backward agriculture and nomadism. The introduction of capitalism into the country in the course of the colonial period has given rise to the creation of new social groups in the urban areas, and accentuated social differences within the traditional rural society towards more clearly delineated social classes.

A. The Traditional Society

The traditional society was composed of settled agriculturalists and pastoral nomads or semi-nomads. These divisions in the mode of existence roughly follow the geographical division of the country into the plateaux and the lowlands: settled agriculture on the highlands and nomadism in the lowlands.

1. Traditional agricultural society

The settled agriculturalists were and remain organised in village communities composed of varying numbers of extended families. The majority of the families who are the original occupants are known as the *restegna*, while those who immigrated into the village later are known as the *makalai ailet*. The prevalent system of land tenure was the *diesa* — communal or village ownership. Every member of the village community had the same rights to use the land. The *diesa* land is divided into three categories according to its fertility. Land from each quality was distributed among the *ghabars* (members of the village) every seven years.

Besides the *diesa*, there also existed the *meriet risti* — family ownership. Here only the members of the extended family had rights of user in the *meriet risti*. This land was not subject to sale without the consent of all the members of the family. And such cases were very rare. In some parts of rural Eritrea, there also existed the *meriet worki* — privately owned land.

In most villages of highland Eritrea, the three land holding systems are to be found. However, the *diesa* is by far the most prevalent. Land was exploited individually and all the instruments of labour were privately owned. As rural highland Eritrea is relatively densely populated, agricultural land is extremely fragmented. Modern agricultural techniques — irrigation, fertilisation, etc. are non-existent.

Most of the settled agriculturalists on the plateaux are christians. The Coptic Church is in fact the owner of a considerable amount of land in this part of the country.

As far as political power is concerned, only the *restegna* had a say in the running of village affairs. The village community was in fact administered by an assembly of elders representing the *restegna* families who are commonly the richest farmers in the village.

2. Traditional nomadic society

The nomadic and semi-nomadic societies in Eritrea are found among several nationalities that inhabit the lowland areas of the country.

Strange as it may seem, it is in these societies that the typical feudal socio-political set-up prevails.

For example, the largely nomadic Beni Amer society in the western lowlands was rigidly divided into two distinct social classes: a ruling aristocracy and a caste of serfs. The Beni Amer nobility called themselves *Nabtab* who in turn acknowledged the supremacy of a paramount chief known as the *Diglal.* The serfs who constitute the overwhelming majority were known as *Tigré.* In spite of common cultural and religious affinities, the division into classes of the Beni Amer is to be originally explained by a complicated history of wars and conquests with the subsequent submission of the *Tigré* and the socio-economic and political superiority of the *Nabtab* who emerged as the 'protectors' of the serf population of the society.

Although the serfs had the right to own livestock, and the grazing lands occupied by the different groups in the society were defined only by habit and tacit traditional agreement, the serfs were nevertheless tied to the *Nabtab* by a series of feudal obligations: tributary payments, regular obligatory gifts and corvée labour. These economic advantages ensured to the overlord a surplus income and his further enrichment. Coupled with his social and political class prerogatives (the social stigma attached to the serfs, their total exclusion from all political life of the society, the exclusive reservation of all menial labour to the serfs, etc.) these privileges were at the base of the feudal character of these societies.

It is to be noted here that even before and after the advent of various colonialisms these societies were ridden with latent or open class contradiction between the landlords and the serfs with the latter seeking to liberate themselves from their feudal ties.

B. Italian colonial domination and its consequences for Eritrean society

Italy established its colonial rule in Eritrea in 1889. Its aims were to make Eritrea a) a settler colony
        b) a base for launching further colonial conquests in the region
        c) a market for its manufactured goods.
These objectives greatly influenced Italy's policy in its first colony.

1. Industrialisation and urbanisation

In the first period of its colonial rule 1889-1930, Italy's policy was to promote new settlement. A number of towns were built and some infrastructural projects: harbours, a system of roads and railroads linking the towns and criss-crossing all the different regions of the country. During this period, industrial development was discouraged for the aim was to make the colony dependent on Italian consumer and manufactured goods. Thus Italy poured capital into Eritrea for its infrastructure, for settlement purposes and for military reasons. These all entailed forced and salaried employment, and thus the first signs of the emergence of a 'multi-national' Eritrean working class.

The second period of Italian colonial policy (1930-1941) was heavily influenced by fascist Italy's expansionist designs in the region. The already existing infrastructure was greatly expanded and new war-related projects were implemented. Massive public works were begun. What characterises this period is the spectacular growth of light industries and the rapid urbanisation of the population. The European population which was barely 5,000 before 1930 increased to 50,000 in 1935. By 1940, about 20% of the entire Eritrean population was urbanised.

2. Italian rural policy

Italian colonialists regarded Eritrea, with its temperate climate, as ideal for their settlement schemes. Settling their 'surplus' population necessarily entailed modifications to economic and social organisation in the rural areas.

In the highlands where settled agriculture was practised, vast areas of the most fertile arable land were expropriated on various pretexts. These lands were simply handed over to Italian settlers for them to set up commercial farms. The area of land for pasture and cultivation was drastically reduced. Peasants in the already densely populated plateau found it difficult to ensure their subsistence way of life. Farming lots that were already parcelised became more and more fragmented. As far as Church land was concerned, the colonial government confiscated most of it and turned it into crown land.

The Italian colonialists also broke up the socio-political set-up of the village communities. They appointed their nominees as village headmen and chiefs in charge of sub-districts. These were mostly from the *restegna* families. This invested some individuals and families with political and administrative power which was eventually to be used as an instrument for their personal enrichment, and their possession of the means of production (land) within the *diesa* (communal) land tenure system.

In the Eritrean lowlands, the colonial government decreed a land statute in 1909, which was subsequently revised in 1926, whereby the low-lying plains — land located below 800 meters altitude (over 50% of of the country) — were declared *terre demaniali* or state lands. In addition, decrees declaring areas of the country as state lands reserved for colonisation were passed. Lands along river courses and other more fertile areas were declared state domains.

Where the feudal mode of production prevailed, all the measures taken by the colonial government were aimed at reinforcing the exploitation of the serfs. The latter, whose living conditions were deteriorating at that time, found that the colonialists openly supported the feudal classes. The Italians found feudal political and social systems well suited to their purposes.

3. The emergence of social classes

Under Italian colonial domination, the living conditions of the Eritrean peasantry became more miserable than ever. Deprived of their land, the peasants were forced to flow into the colonial centres to make a living by selling their labour power to Italian capital.

The *proletariat:* the Eritrean working class, composed of the wage earners employed in the infrastructure and public works, light industries, commercial and distribution services and in the commercial farms, was multinational in composition and developed a sharp sense of common identity in the course of its inhuman exploitation by Italian capital. Under Italian fascism, workers had no rights whatsoever. Fascist colonial legislation forbade the formation of associations and trade unions. The brutal oppression of the working class, coupled with an official colour bar, meant its reaction to fascist policies was sporadic and unsustained.

The *peasantry:* With the deterioration of his subsistence production, the Eritrean peasant had either to migrate to the towns or to be recruited by the colonial army to serve as cannon fodder in the Italian wars of conquest – 60,000 Eritreans fought in Libya alone.

With his land confiscated and in danger of being uprooted from his society, the Eritrean peasant did not react passively to colonial rule. This period is marked by a number of peasant uprisings and a general atmosphere of rebellion which obliged the colonial government to give up a number of its settlement projects.

Since the *diesa* landholding system, the rights of users in communal land did not necessitate the physical presence of every member of the village, all those who left for the towns or joined the colonial army retained their rights over the land. As a result, there arose the phenomenon of absentee 'users' of land. These usually made arrangements with their relatives or others who could cultivate their plots on their behalf. As a consequence, a number of farmers began to farm the plots alloted to them and those of the absentee members of the village *ghebars.* Such a practice has been the basis of the social and economic differentiation among the peasantry in rural Eritrea.

The *intelligentsia:* During the Italian occupation, there were practically no social services for the indigenous population. Medical services were limited to the Italian settler colony. Education was deliberately restricted. This confidential directive given to Italian headmasters by the director of education in Eritrea in 1938 speaks for itself:

> By the end of the fourth year, the Eritrean student should be able to speak our language moderately well. He should know the four

arithmetical operations within normal limits . . . And history – he should know only the names of those who made Italy great.

Nevertheless, a handful of Eritreans were trained to become interpreters, low level clerks, etc. These constituted a small intelligentsia, the nucleus of the future bureaucracy and of the petty bourgeois class in the country.

C. British colonial administration and its impact on Eritrean society

We can discern two distinct periods in the British rule of Eritrea. The British occupied Eritrea in 1941, at a time when the Second World War was raging. From then up to the end of the war, the British, without making any change in the socio-economic structure left by the Italians, set out instead to fully exploit military facilities and industrial establishments built by the ex-colonial power for war purposes. In order to supply the Allied forces with consumer goods, the British began immediately to exploit the abundant skilled labour and resources of the country. In a short period of three years, over 300 factories were set up. This period of British rule is therefore characterised by the over-exploitation of the Eritrean working class and the accumulation of super-profits by British colonialism and Italian capital.

However, the end of the war in 1945 brought about a drastic change in British economic policy in Eritrea. The forced boom came to a sudden halt. A number of factories closed down. We know that in the discussions about the disposition of Eritrea, the British presented their scheme for a partition of Eritrea. One of their arguments in support of this plan was that an independent Eritrea would not be economically viable; and as though to substantiate their argument they started to ruin the Eritrean economy. A great number of buildings and factories were dismantled. Some industrial hardware and infrastructural equipment were transferred to other British colonies.

What then were the consequences of British rule for the Eritrean social classes?

The *working class:* During the early period of British colonialism, the size of the working class increased tremendously. There was a further drain of the rural population towards the urban centres. But with the accelerated exploitation of the workers, their living conditions did not improve at all. Worse still, with the later closing down of factories and the calling off of infrastructural works, the working class was faced with mass unemployment. The once urbanised Eritrea population could not return to the countryside. The working class was thus literally faced with starvation. It began to rise up against British colonial rule. Organised in trade unions at factory level, workers began to wage struggles to improve their miserable living conditions. It was not long before they started to play an active role in the intense political movement of this period.

The *peasantry:* The misery of life in the towns was paralleled by a major deterioration of living conditions in rural Eritrea. As we have already pointed out, the British had left intact the socio-economic structure set up by the Italian colonialists. In fact, they proceeded with the further expropriation of vast areas of the most fertile land from the peasantry and gave it to Italian capitalist farmers. What's more, they increased greatly the taxes levied on the peasants. As life in the towns became increasingly difficult, the workers began to depend on the countryside for food aid in order to feed their families. It should be remembered that the veterans of the ex-colonial army had returned to the villages. All these factors made subsistence life in the country-side more precarious.

In the highlands, Eritrean peasants reacted vigorously against this state of affairs. They were especially indignant at the expropriation of their land. They organised armed attacks on Italian farms and burned them to the ground. Many Italian capitalist farmers were killed and had their heads chopped off.

In lowland Eritrea and the areas where feudalism held sway, the class struggle between the serfs and the feudal landlords reached its highest stage. For eight years (1942-1949), a powerful anti-feudal movement swept the lowlands. The serfs who constituted over 90% of the population openly revolted against the feudal landlords, refusing to pay taxes and dues, and demanding complete emancipation from their masters. Although this self-emancipation movement was very strong, the serfs could not win their total liberation. However, the British colonial administration had to take account of it. More important still, this movement seriously shook the economic and political base of the *shumagles* and the *Nabtab* chiefs.

Faced with peasant uprisings and social upheaval all over rural Eritrea, the colonial administration tried to strengthen the political and administrative apparatus in the countryside.

The *urban petty bourgeoisie:* With the general degradation of the socio-economic situation, the lot of the urban petty bourgeoisie also worsened. It should be remembered that when the British attacked the Italian forces, they presented themselves as the 'liberators' of the Eritrean people and as such they had its whole-hearted and active support. However, the reality proved to be something else. The fascist political and administrative machinery remained. The embryonic Eritrean intelligentsia that emerged under Italian colonialism had expected changes and entertained the hope of occupying the posts held by the Italians. It was disappointed, even though its size increased significantly due to the greater access to education under British rule. Moreover, after the end of the second world war, the urban petty bourgeoisie also experienced mass unemployment. Many who tried to eke out a living by starting small businesses were refused licences. Thus, the urban petty bourgeoisie ended up in a state of total agitation. It organised demonstrations, published articles and conducted other struggles against British colonialism.

Given this critical socio-economic situation all sections of Eritrean society saw only one solution to their problems: independence. By this time, economic and political integration was already completed, and Eritreans of different nationalities, ethnic groups and religions were waging a common struggle based on their common exploitation and humiliation. In order to pursue their scheme of partitioning Eritrea, British colonialism had to resort to other means. It is here that Haïle Selassie's feudal regime comes into the picture. Since its interests coincided with those of the British, they both set out to break the common anti-colonial struggle in Eritrea by first of all fomenting religious and national animosities, secondary but visible contradictions among the Eritrean people.

D. End of British rule and political upsurge in Eritrea

This period is characterised by intense political activity in the country. In the little that is written about this period, political movements and parties are analysed in religious or national terms. A closer look at the social bases of some of the contending parties is however required.

The Unionist Party: Reportedly the Party of the christian and highland people of Eritrea, we know today that the Unionist Party was mainly the creation of the Ethiopian imperial regime. In order to create a pro-Ethiopian public opinion, which did not then exist spontaneously, the Ethiopian regime first turned to the Coptic Church. Why? The Coptic Church had been dispossessed of its large estates by the Italians. Under the British administration, the Church had made several unsuccessful petitions demanding the restitution of this land. Thus, when the Ethiopian regime promised the return of the land if the two countries were to be united, the hierarchy of the Church soon became a supporter of such a union. Once assured of the support of the Church, Haile Selassie's regime next turned to the higher sections of the petty bourgeoisie. These social groups who consituted the small Eritrean intelligentsia during Italian colonialism and whose hopes and ambitions, as we have seen above, were frustrated by the British were lured into the Party by promises of jobs and status in the Union. They became the organisers and the leaders of the Unionist Party.

We would like to stress that the Unionist Party found another of its main bases in the feudal classes, particularly the landed aristocrats of the western lowlands of Moslem Eritrea. We have seen to what extent the powerful emancipation movement of the serfs constituted a threat to those interests. Not surprisingly these feudalists saw Ethiopia's feudal regime as a staunch protector.

The Unionist Party therefore represented the interest of these three classes. Their call for unity with Ethiopia based on historical and national factors can hardly disguise their real class motivations. Otherwise, it would be difficult to explain why many of the upper petty bourgeois unionists and leaders of the Party, once their interests were fulfilled in the federal set-up, became its ardent defenders and fought against the Ethiopian regime's schemes of total annexation. Similarly, if it were not for class interests, how could we explain the fact that the moslem aristocracy became one of the major forces of a party instigated by the Coptic Church? A party like this one is determined by the interests it serves and by the social groups that dominate the society. It does not mean the Unionist Party did not have a mass following. The influence of the Church over the highland peasants was great and became very important in creating a consensus among them. Nor did the Church hesitate to use the threat of excommunication against the advocates of independence.

The Moslem League and the Liberal Progressive Party: These were the main organisations fighting for independence. As to their social bases, we know that the Moslem League emanated from the anti-feudal movement of the serfs of the lowlands. As we mentioned earlier, the movement's calls for emancipation from serfdom and for national independence were inseparable. The Party was founded and led by a bourgeois nationalist of serf origin with a great influence among the serfs. The Liberal Progressive Party, though it enjoyed the support of the urban proletariat, drew its membership from and was dominated by the lower petty bourgeoisie and the urban intellectuals of the highlands.

It has to be pointed out that though these two parties expressed the aspirations of the masses, their leadership was in the hands of the petty bourgeoisie and even of certain feudal elements. It is thus understandable that they were not resolute enough in their positions and were disposed to make compromises at critical moments of the independence struggle.

E. Eritrean society under Ethiopian colonialism

The 'Federation' with Ethiopia was virtually imposed on Eritrea by a UN decision which meant in fact the negation of its right to self-determination. Once it occupied Eritrea what did the Ethiopian regime set out to do? The anomaly in the supposed co-existence of democratic and autonomous Eritrea with an autocratic and archaic Ethiopian regime quickly became evident.

In order to destroy the political life of Eritrea, the Ethiopian regime set out to cripple the economy of the country. It expropriated one of the major revenue sources, Eritrea's share of customs duties. Several factories were dismantled, closed down and simply transferred to Ethiopia. The regime went so far as to adopt a deliberate policy of blocking the further industrial development of the country.

On the political level, Haile Selassie's regime also suppressed freedom of speech, of press and of association. Journalists and intellectuals were imprisoned. It stripped the Eritrean Assembly of all the powers with which it had been vested. It subverted the country's judicial system. It lowered the Eritrean national flag.

On the cultural plane, it suppressed the Eritrean languages and forcibly imposed Amharic as the only and official language of the country. The Ethiopian regime did not even hesitate to burn books written in Tigrinya.

These measures of systematically liquidating Eritrean autonomy had their impact on the different classes.

The *working class:* With the Ethiopian regime's moves to ruin the economy and to annex the country politically, the Federation period (1952-62) was characterised by the complete weakening of the working class but by an unprecedented growth of the worker's movement. At the end of 1952, the workers founded the General Union of Labour Syndicates to enable them to continue their political struggle. The Ethiopian regime could not tolerate the creation of such an organisation, and set out to destroy it. Government agents shot and wounded the Union's president, who had been a founder of the Liberal Progressive Party. He was subsequently banished from the country. The workers were prohibited from holding any assembly. The Union's newspaper was banned. The movement went underground and by 1957, in alliance with the Eritrean students, it spread political agitation all over the country. This active political work reached its peak in the calling of a general strike in 1958 which paralysed all the major Eritrean towns for several days. In these massive demonstrations, the workers, students and other sections of the population condemned Ethiopian economic plunder and openly demanded Eritrea's independence. The Ethiopian regime reacted with brute force, killing and wounding hundreds and imprisoning thousands of demonstrators.

These repressive measures proved a set back in the organisation of the workers for many years to come. They accelerated the emigration of Eritrean workers to other countries. Although Eritrean workers never ceased in their support for the independence struggle as members or by raising funds, their movement was at a low ebb when the armed struggle started.

The rise of a *bourgeoisie:* We have seen which sections of urban society advocated Eritrea coming under Ethiopian domination and why. After its installation in Eritrea, the Ethiopian regime fulfilled the promises it had made to the upper petty bourgeoisie. It bestowed economic advantages and titles on them. Adding corruption to the grant of privileges by the Emperor, they began to amass sizeable personal wealth. For its loyal service, the upper petty bourgeoisie had landed property made over to it: buildings, villas, land in the towns, formerly in the hands of the British colonial authority.

Some businesses formerly held by Italians were also tranferred to them. With the financial wealth they accumulated, others started new businesses. Gradually, they became the owners of factories, commercial firms, insurance and transport companies. The same classes occupied the high posts in the bureaucracy, the military and the police forces, which were in turn a fertile ground for the consolidation of their economic and financial power.

With the introduction of international capital into the country, these former upper echelons of the petty bourgeoisie ended up becoming a solid and clearly delineated bourgeois class. The development of this bourgeoisie was not of course smooth and linear. The upper petty bourgeois unionists who became the defenders of the Federation were either bought off by the regime, liquidated, forced to leave the country or obliged to distance themselves from the regime. These last ones were replaced by others more loyal and content with the economic benefits they were deriving from the system.

The *urban petty bourgeoisie:* during the Ethiopia period, this class swelled in size. Estimated to be about 20% of the population, it is the most important group of the Eritrean urban population. The lower sections of the petty bourgeoisie felt feudal Ethiopia's political and economic oppression and the exploitation of international capital as much as anyone.

In the 1950's, the students fought strongly against the violation of national and democratic rights. After the bloody massacre of 1958, mentioned above, they played an active role in the clandestine organisation known as the Mahber Showate that was subsequently formed to prepare for an armed struggle. From this period up to the seventies, the Eritrean students inside and outside the country have done propaganda and agitation work of mobilisation and organisation in favour of independence. Revolutionary students and intellectuals were among the first to join the armed struggle.

Rural Society: The imperial Ethiopian regime had its inevitable consequences on rural Eritrea: the consolidation of feudalism where it existed, and its introduction in the other areas, plus the degradation of subsistence and the pauperisation of the peasant masses.

The *feudal landlord class:* The support feudal landlords gave to the Unionist Party was rewarded by Haile Selassie's regime. The *Shumagles, Nabtab* chiefs of the lowlands, now more secure in their positions of privilege, had aristocratic titles and property bestowed on them. Many were appointed to high posts in the bureaucracy. In the Eritrean highlands, the loyalty of the feudal elements was rewarded by strengthening of their political and administrative power. This became an important source of their economic strength. It enabled them to tamper with the *diesa* landholding system and to dominate commercial activities in the countryside. In addition, with new economic advantages and with their administrative power, they began to move to the towns and to hold business interests there. Hence, the feudalists of the highlands eventually constituted themselves a distinct social group. With their growing interests in the urban centres, many of the landlords of both highlands and lowlands became more and more absentee landlords.

II THE IMPACT OF THE LIBERATION ON THE STRUCTURE OF ERITREAN SOCIETY

A. The nationalist and social dimensions of the liberation struggle

We have already noted that the liberation struggle had been defined by the EPLF as both a national and a social venture. This characterisation is the outcome of intense political struggles within the Eritrean liberation movement. The bitter debates that were waged within the ELF in the second half of the sixties and which culminated in the birth of the EPLF in 1970 revolved around the character, the objectives and motive forces of the revolution (see the various testimonies to this effect indicated in the bibliography.) When we analyse this evolution, we notice that with the birth of this front the struggle became clearly defined as 'national' and 'democratic'. The elements in the ELF who were eventually to be found in the EPLF came to the conclusion that the only path to victory was to struggle on two fronts: that for national independence, and also for the profound transformation of the society in the democratic sense. According to the analysis made by the EPLF, these two phases of the liberation struggle are so closely interwoven that it is impossible to separate one from the other. The popular aspirations for independence could not be fulfilled unless, in the course of the liberation struggle, the exploitative structures of society were transformed in favour of the basic interests of the majority of the people. And on the other hand, the EPLF thought that it was futile to think of meeting the basic demands of the masses, the main force of the revolution, outside the context of an independent Eritrea.

The synthesis between national independence and social liberation is the main topic of this paper. We can see here a similarity between the process that the liberation struggle has undergone and that which took place in the Portuguese colonies at the same stage of its history. The obstinate, brutal and backward nature of the colonial power, the incapacity of the coloniser to bring about any neo-colonial solution, and to a certain extent the failure of the experiences of the newly independent African countries, convinced the liberation movements in these countries that in order to advance, the liberation struggle should be solidly based on the exploited masses and serve their interests; that there can not be political independence without economic independence; and that the national struggle (independence) and the revolutionary struggle (economic independence and social transformation of backward societies) should be one and the same, and waged simultaneously. All these hold true in the Eritrean case, except that here the magnitude of these factors had to be further underlined, and other factors specific to the Eritrea situation added.

There are three series of factors we would like to mention. First, the fact that imperialist interests were not only the causes of the struggle for national liberation, but these same forces persisted in their negation of Eritrea's right to self-determination either by their direct participation in the repression of the struggle or by their open hostility, their indifference or by their attempts to make use of it. Second, by virtue of its feudal and totally dependent nature, the enemy that confronted the Eritrean fighters was much more backward, brutal and completely devoid of any chance of solving Eritrean problems. Thirdly, one must note the grave errors, defects and failures of the first years of the armed struggle. At this period, despite popular support, the leadership of the liberation movement was dominated by feudal elements, who sought to gain independence by a quick route and in the shortest span of time. However, the contradictions within the ELF, plus Eritrean political and socio-economic conditions as well as the world situation, did not allow the liberation struggle any choice but that of following the strategy of a protracted people's war as the only path towards any advancement of the revolution. This was the analysis of the founders of the EPLF and it was adopted as the new political line of the organisation.

B. The EPLF's views on social classes, their attitudes and their role in the revolution

In breaking away from the Eritrean Liberation Front, the EPLF saw as the fundamental task of the Eritrean revolution the definition of the existing social contradiction. The EPLF found the main cause of the serious setbacks that the liberation struggle had encountered under the leadership of the ELF was a lack of analysis of Eritrean society, the determination of its various classes and their attitudes towards the revolution.

In order to understand better the structural changes in the society that the EPLF aims at, it is necessary to have a look at the way the movement defines its 'friends and enemies' in the ongoing struggle. In brief, the enemies of the revolution are colonialism, imperialism and feudalism; on the opposite side its motive forces are the working class, the peasantry, the urban petty bourgeoisie and other patriotic groups. But let us go into further detail and see things from the point of view of each of the social classes which are respectively the targets of the struggle and the forces of transformation as identified by the EPLF.

1. The social targets of the revolution

The *feudal class:* in an investigation of Eritrean rural society in the highlands conducted by the EPLF and published in 1975, the Front bases the determination of the social classes in the countryside on the ownership of the means of production (land) and of farm implements. They do not participate in production and exploit the labour force of the tenants. A feudal landlord is one who owns more than eight *tsimdi* (a measurement of land — a plot that a pair of oxen can plough in one day under normal conditions) and more than four pairs of oxen. He uses the services of several tenants. Usury is a common practice of the feudalists. By lending at very high rates to the poverty stricken peasants, they derive substantial income. As to the feudalist in lowland Eritrea, we have briefly mentioned their exploitation of the tenants.

The monopoly of the economic and commercial life of the rural areas by this class needs to be recalled here. We have already seen that the feudal class has always been linked with Italian and British colonialism and was greatly consolidated by the Ethiopian feudal regime. Hence, it is evident that it has no interest in the success of the liberation struggle and that it is by its very nature hostile to any social revolution. The EPLF has identified this class as the undoubted target of the revolution.

The *upper section of the bourgeoisie:* we have previously dealt with the formation of this class and its role in Eritrean society. According to the EPLF, the upper section of the bourgeoisie is composed of the comprador bourgeoisie and the bureaucratic capitalists. As is the case in all neo-colonial countries, it serves as an agent of international capital and is heading the import-export trade, the financial institutions and the industrial and agricultural concerns. It has always actively opposed Eritrea's independence struggle. As a stumbling block to the social revolution, the Front fights for its overthrow.

The *national bourgeoisie:* This class is very small in number and in weight. The history of the struggle shows that a minority of this class have given wavering support to the movement while the majority has remained neutral. Consequently, the EPLF takes a prudent stance towards it.

2. The motive forces of the revolution

The *working class:* we have said that despite the Eritrean working class's record of militancy particularly in the years preceeding the country's annexation, the armed struggle was launched at a time when the workers' movement was seriously weakened. A large section of this class was to be subsequently dispersed throughout neighbouring countries. It is known that the ELF did not undertake any work of organising the working class and providing it with leadership. With the formation of the EPLF, the worker-peasant alliance was defined as 'the basis of the Eritrean revolution' and the working class, being in the best objective conditions to generate a social consciousness, 'the vanguard of the revolution'.

What is the EPLF's analysis of this class? As compared to the peasantry, the Eritrean working class is very small. It is composed of an industrial and an agricultural proletariat. Inside Eritrea, the former are in manufacturing industry, construction, communications and the service industries. The latter are mostly in the big plantations run by foreign capital. The wages and working conditions in Eritrea were as low as in other countries that are economically dependent. As a class, the proletariat, even if it was not very numerous, has always been in a social relation of direct exploitation. As in most neo-colonial countries, the majority of the Eritrean workers are of peasant origin and maintain close ties with the countryside. This is seen as a positive factor for the forging of the worker-peasant alliance.

The EPLF sees the key to the success of the Eritrean struggle in 'the unity of all patriotic classes based on the worker-peasant alliance and under the leadership of the working class'. This could be just a slogan, as has been heard in many places. However, it has concrete implications in the actual policy of the EPLF. This is the reason for the effort exerted in organising the workers as a class in order to enable it to play its proper role in the revolution. We will examine this later on.

The *peasantry:* to the EPLF, the peasantry (settled agriculturists, nomads, and semi-nomads) constitutes the main force of the revolution. Besides being the overwhelming majority of the population, it is the most exploited class. The peasants lead a wretched life and are consequently the most reliable allies of the working class.

The *peasantry of the highlands:* the EPLF's above mentioned investigation of Eritrean highland society shows that the peasantry is not a homogeneous entity. In the determination of this class (according to ownership of land and of farm implements and draught animals), we find that it is divided into poor, middle and rich peasants.

The *poor peasants.* In terms of size, they are the most important group (about 60% of the peasantry). Land is, of course, their main problem. However, since among the poor peasants there are those who own a small plot of land and a few farm implements, and others who own almost no means of production except their labour power, they can be divided into four categories.

The first category include those who have their own labour power, one ox and a small plot of land. In order to avoid renting oxen from feudalists and rich peasants and thus giving away part of their produce, they usually make arrangements whereby they lend each other their oxen. If not, they have no choice but to rent oxen, which frequently happens.

The second category is composed of those who have their labour power, a small plot and some farm implements. Having no oxen, they rent them from the landlords and the rich peasants.

In the third category, we find those who only own a small plot of land. These are people who are aged, orphaned, plus widowed or divorced women. Hence, they are necessarily obliged to rent out their plot to people who can farm it. Depending on the arrangement, they receive a third or one half of the meagre produce.

In the fourth category are people who own nothing but their labour power: the young or unmarried, the newly married or those who reside in the village but are not the original members of the community. Hence, to eke out a living of pure subsistence, they either rent land or sell their labour power to the rich peasants or the feudalists.

It is not difficult to see that the life led by the poor peasants is one of abject misery. Their farm produce cannot last them for one year. They are consequently the victims of usury and other forms of exploitation. To ensure their subsistence, they look for jobs in towns and on plantations during certain periods of the year. Since they have nothing to lose, they constitute a strong base for the liberation struggle. Poor peasants are the first to demand land reform and to defend it tenaciously.

The *middle peasants:* next to the poor peasants, they are numerically the most important (about 30% of the peasantry). A middle peasant is one who owns eight *tsimdi* of land, a pair of oxen and a few domestic animals. He participates in production. Some of the poor peasants, in fact, do rent land and sell their labour power and are thus exploited by land and interest rates. As a whole, the middle peasants do not hire farm labour. Although they are not obliged to migrate to the urban centres during the off-seasons, they make but subsistence livelihood. As regards their attitude towards the revolutionary struggle, the middle peasants see that their interests will be better served with the success of the revolution. They participate in the revolution, particularly when it scores successes. The EPLF believes that the middle peasantry is an important force and that the revolution has to bid for its support by carrying out the careful work of conscientisation.

The *rich peasants:* a rich peasant owns more than eight *tsimdi* of land and over two pairs of oxen. He owns better and more farm implements. He farms the extensive land that he owns or rents himself. However, he hires farm labour in addition or leases part of his land or implements to poor peasants. Rich peasants lend out money at high rates of interest. They dominate the administration of community affairs. This enables them to accumulate surplus which in its turn provides them with the material capacity for improving their land. As a whole, according to the analysis of the EPLF, the rich peasantry is and can be patriotic in its attitude. However, a thoroughgoing social revolution and an eventual change in the structure of the society is objectively a threat to its privileges. For this reason, its support is not consistent. The EPLF recognises the need to pursue a prudent policy in dealing with the rich peasantry.

The *nomads of the lowlands:* Last but not least is the nomadic and semi-nomadic population of Eritrea. We have already seen something of their historical development and referred to their socio-economic conditions. Besides being, in terms of size, a very important section of the rural masses, the nomads are not only among the most exploited but are, in addition, the most neglected group of the Eritrean rural society. As for the pastoral semi-nomadic people, they are exploited for they have to rent land for grazing and cultivation from the feudalists or the Ethiopian regime. Heavy taxes are levied upon them. In addition, the landlords exact various services from them such as, corvée labour and tribute payments. The EPLF considers them a very strong force for the revolution. In fact, we have seen the role they played in the independence struggle. They are the ones that have supported the armed struggle from the very beginning and thus have suffered heavily from the repression of the Ethiopian regime.

The *urban petty bourgeoisie:* In the EPLF's class analysis, the urban petty bourgeoisie includes the small traders, small scale manufacturers, the intelligentsia (intellectuals, teachers and students), lower government officials, office clerks, lower army and police officers, etc., and constitutes the largest section of the urban population. Except for a thin layer which was either neutral or allied to the Ethiopian regime — this class has played an active role in the national and democratic struggles. However, the EPLF, basing itself on the Eritrean struggle's past experiences, never ceases to point out the dangers in this class's domination of the struggle and also in the lack of awareness of the negative tendencies characteristic of the petty bourgeoisie in the course of the revolution. The EPLF believes that although this class is a reliable ally of the oppressed masses, the revolution cannot achieve its real aims unless it is solidly based on the worker-peasant alliance under the direction of the working class.

It is just such an analysis of the Eritrean society that the EPLF set out in order to prepare the necessary transformations of the structures of society. However, the questions which remain to be treated are, on the one hand, whether the praxis of the movement corresponds to its theory, and on the other, the means by which this aim has been pursued.

C. Changes in Social Structure in the Liberated Areas

From its birth, the EPLF linked the struggle of the Eritrean people for national independence intimately to the struggle for its social liberation. It was henceforth to be waged for the establishment of a sovereign and socialist Eritrean society. To this end, the Front adopted the strategy of a self-reliant protracted people's war as the only way to achieve these goals. This waging of a self-reliant protracted people's war required profound changes in existing Eritrean society. For the EPLF, it meant that several tasks had to be accomplished on different fronts. It had to obtain the total and conscious participation of the masses in the ongoing struggle; they had to be organised, politicised and armed. In addition, the EPLF had to lead them in doing away with exploitative and archaic production relations, fetters to any development of the productive forces. It had to encourage and to prepare the ground for the eventual conquest of political power by the oppressed classes that constitute the social base of the revolution. In short, class struggle had to be waged simultaneously with that for national liberation. How did the EPLF go about this? Let us look at the measures taken by the Front in the rural areas and towns under its control.

Land reform and the transformation of the social structure in the countryside.

First, we must see the conditions under which the EPLF began and carried out its revolutionary work among the peasant masses. The difficult years following its formation and the break out of the civil war in 1972 did not allow the Front to implement its political line effectively. Thus, the mobilisation of the masses in general could not start before the end of 1974. The experiences we will study here date from that time and they were made in extremely difficult military and political situations. In order to grasp the real dimension of any social transformation, it has to be viewed in context. Land reform by itself does not, for example, necessarily imply the profound transformation (in a socialist sense) of the production relations or of class relations in a given society. Hence, an understanding of the real implications of land reform in the liberated areas in Eritrea requires that it be first placed in the overall revolutionary situation that prevails in the country. Secondly, it necessitates a closer examination of its direct effects on the social set-up of the society in question. To better serve this latter purpose, we will look at two case studies of land reform in two village communities of the highlands: Azien and Medri Zien.

   Azien. Azien is a typical village of the Eritrean plateau situated a few kilometers north of Asmara. A medium sized village, its land holding system is that of *diesa*.But like most villages in this area, Azien underwent the social process that we have described above. That is, feudal elements using the political power given to them and consolidated by the successive colonialists had prevented the *diesa* system from functioning. The distribution of the land which, according to this system, had to take place every seven years was long overdue. By 1975, thirty-eight years had elapsed since the last redistribution of land. With the passing of the years, the landlords and the rich peasants acquired a considerable amount of land and by the mechanisms analysed above, they exploited the poor peasants. By the time the EPLF forces arrived in the village, large tracts of land had virtually become the private property of the landlords and of the rich peasants. Communal village ownership had almost turned into *de facto* private ownership. The number of the landless and poor peasants thus went on increasing and they became the overwhelming majority of the peasants. In these thirty-eight years, the peasant masses of Azien continuously demanded the

application of the *diesa* system. At the local level, their demands were
blocked by those elements who monopolised economic and political
power. At the higher level, their demands were simply dismissed as ille-
gitimate or rejected.

By the time, the EPLF forces set foot in Azien (towards the end of
1974), the peasants were ready for the abolition of the existing order,
the source of their plight. But it was only after a year that the land
reform was carried out. How did the EPLF go about reorganising the
liberated zones? For the EPLF liberating a zone does not simply mean
driving out the enemy from a given part of the country. Before launch-
ing a military operation, the Front makes a detailed study of the historical, political and socio-economic conditions of the zone and makes the
necessary preparations beforehand for the later organisation of the
liberated zone. At the end of the battle, the EPLF would bring into the
zone all the units in charge of different departments (education, health,
etc.), together with those fighters of the People's army who would have
to defend the liberated zone from any enemy attack.

In Azien, in response to the peasants' demands, armed propaganda
units set out to prepare the ground for the eventual transformation of
the socio-economic conditions of the village. These cadres of the
Department of Mass Organisation made, as an initial step, a careful
study not only of the general socio-economic conditions of the village
but also the socio-economic status of each peasant household. These
studies constitute the basis upon which the Front identifies the poor
peasants in particular in order to organise them in secret cells*. The
EPLF believes that it is only when the peasants are organised that they
can lead the revolutionary struggle forward. The Front is convinced
that the struggle for social transformation should be the act of the
peasant masses themselves. It is only in the process of a revolutionary
struggle which the oppressed peasant masses carry out by themselves
and for themselves, that they can be liberated from all feudal relations.
An authentic revolution can never be declared from above.

However, before setting up the cells composed of the poor and to
a certain extent of the middle peasants, the propaganda unit cadres
called a series of meetings attended by all the members of the village,
which furnished a comprehensive political education ranging from
Eritrea's history to the aims of the present revolution. Additional
private contacts and discussions were made with poor and middle
peasants. In the course of the meetings and discussions, the most recep-
tive peasants were recruited into secret cells of up to 15 members.

At this stage of the revolutionary struggle the only way to break
up the feudal type of production relations that had established itself
in the village communities of the Eritrean highlands is to return to the
strict observation of the *diesa*, communal village ownership system.

* Their secret character is in order to avoid open social confrontations at this
  stage.

This tradition more or less assures the socialisation of the ownership of land. With this aim in mind, the problem of land use and ownership is frequently brought up in the discussions of the secret cells. Since it is what they had been trying to do for decades, the proposal for the redistribution of land is very strongly supported by the members of the cells when it is brought up.

However, before putting forward such proposals in public, the EPLF believes that steps have to be taken beforehand to change the power relations in the administration of village affairs, in the village assembly. It is this assembly that organises the redistribution of land. We would like to recall here that, although in principle the leaders of the village assembly were democratically elected, they in fact came almost exclusively from the *restegna* families, and excluded the *makelai ailet* for instance. With the evolution in the class composition of the highland Eritrean leadership, the village assemblies naturally became the preserve of the landlords and the rich peasants. It is evident that any carrying out of land redistribution assumes a previous change in the class character of the village assembly. Thus, in the EPLF held areas, the work of the redistribution of land usually began with the agitation of the organised peasants for new elections for leadership to the village assemblies in the weekly meetings of the latter.

It should be noted here that women have participated for the first time in the history of rural Eritrea in the political life of the village communities (assemblies, elections, redistribution of land, etc.). Women's clandestine cells have also been set-up and their members play an important part in the process of the social transformation of village life. The general political mobilisation of the village together with the active participation of the members of the poor peasants' cells and those of women show their effects in the results of the new elections. Members of sections of the peasantry who either for economic reasons (poor and landless peasants) or socio-historical ones (the non-original inhabitants, e.g. the *Makelai ailet)* were hitherto excluded from access to posts of responsibility in the village assemblies now acquire political and administrative power. The EPLF believes that this fundamental change in the class relations of the village community is a pre-condition for the proper carrying out of land reform, which in its initial stage is based on the equal redistribution of land according to the traditional land tenure system.

Azien underwent this same process. By the end of November 1975, there were six clandestine cells composed of seventy members, the majority of them landless and poor peasants. With the agitation work and the active participation of the latter and the Front's cadres, a new leading body, the majority of whom were organised peasants, was elected to run village affairs. Subsequently, the question of redistribution of land was brought up in public debates attended by over 1,200 peasants. It got their overwhelming support without much difficulty.

Another committee of nine members was then elected to lay the ground work — this after 38 years — for the redistribution of the land. In a report presented by the committee, it was found that 1,500 households were eligible for participation in the redistribution in a medium-sized village like Azien that had a little less than 5,000 inhabitants. After excluding 300 for various reasons (those who had not cultivated their land for the last five years, those who were serving in the Ethiopian army and fighting against the revolution, etc.) a list of 1,200 beneficiaries was established.

Medri-Zien. The following example of land reform in the village of Medri-Zien demonstrates the EPLF's firm determination to side with the masses in their struggle to break feudal relations, even in difficult circumstances. The Coptic Church has always been a feudal institution in rural Eritrea, and the Debre-Sina monastery was no exception. It owned almost all the land of the nearby village of Medri-Zien with 500 peasant households. The peasants of this village worked for the monastery as tenants and kept one-third of their crop. The peasants of Medri-Zien had for long demanded that the land be collectively owned by the village. The monastery's chief priest had always refused, thus causing constant conflict between the peasant masses of Medri-Zien and the monastery. At times clashes broke out and when they got out of hand the monastery had recourse to the Ethiopian army.

In this struggle, the EPLF supported the demands of the peasants. As the conflict sharpened, the EPLF launched a campaign in favour of the tenants' demands. Cells of the Peasant Association were formed in Medri-Zien and a village assembly was established. It was not long before this class struggle involved the entire region. Thus, the only thing the Church could do was to arouse public sentiment against the Front by branding it as anti-religious. But this was to no avail. The tenants of Medri-Zien, supported by the peasant masses of the region and by the EPLF, were so firm in their demands that this provoked a division within the monastery which gradually lead to the isolation of the chief monks. The monastery had to give up and today the land of Medre-Zien is under the *diesa* system.

Besides offering an example of a revolutionary struggle against such a well established feudal institution as the Coptic Church, interesting in this case is the stand of the ELF. When the chief monks saw that they were about to loose their feudal ownership of the land of Medri-Zien, they appealed to the ELF to help them out in their struggle against the tenants. The ELF went to the support of the monastery going so far as to threaten the tenants with arms so that they would restore the land to the monastery. The ELF has done little to transform social structures. It says that it is opposed to the carrying out of land reform at the present stage of the struggle, it should be postponed until after independence. It considers the EPLF's policy in this domaine as 'ultra-leftist'. As to the power relations in the villages under its control, we find practically no change. In these villages, the ELF has set up a five man committee to run the community's affairs. The members of these committees are almost invariably from among the landlords and rich peasants.

What should be stressed is that while basing the land reform on the traditional land tenure system, the EPLF has given the system a new, democratic content. The laws of the customary system have been modified on many points. Previously, it was only the family household that participated in the redistribution of the land. Under the modified system, the members of the village get their plot of land as individuals. This enables the unmarried and the women to have their own plots. We may recall that the latter constituted an important percentage of the landless peasants. It was said above that members of the village who migrated to urban centres retained their right over the use of land and thus left their share of land to be cultivated by the rich peasants and the landlords. In the new redistribution of land, no plots of land are allocated for absentee members of the village unless it is proved that they depend heavily for their living on the produce of the farms. However, some parts of the village land were formally kept in reserve in the event that some of these absentees would decide to come back to live in the village and farm their plots of land.

An example of the drastic measures land reform sometimes involved is offered by the village of Zager, where ninety plots of land that belonged to absentee landlords and collaborators were expropriated and turned over to the village to be farmed collectively. This type of distribution of land eliminates the basis for the accumulation of land by the upper strata of the peasantry and in turn the landlessness and exploitation of the poor peasants. These landless peasants who now have their own plots of land will be less obliged to sell their labour power. On the other hand, with the redistribution of land, plus the Front's very strict ban on usury and control over the commercial activities in the liberated zones, the feudalists and the rich peasants will now be deprived of their main sources of economic and financial power. However, in order for the new beneficiaries of the land reform to be free from exploitation, they will have to have the necessary farm implements and sufficient draught animals — one of the principal causes of class differentiation in rural Eritrea. What is more, despite the land reform's effects of democratising rural life, land for cultivation still remains extremely fragmented. The methods of agriculture are still backward and productivity low. Thus the EPLF is correct in its conviction that the present land reform, though a fundamental initial step towards the profound transformation of the society, cannot be completed without the beginning of collective farming. To this end, the Front has undertaken a vast educational programme. The people's army helps the peasants in their work and assists them to adopt modern methods of farming. Some of the small nationalised commercial farms are made to run on that basis.

Another aspect of land reform carried out by the EPLF is the nationalisation of big mechanised farms and plantations formerly in the hands of the Ethiopian regime of occupation, foreign capitalists and Eritrean collaborators. We will only briefly mention that the Front is also expanding the areas under cultivation and taking up large-scale farming on land expropriated from the enemy. For the time being, these farms are run by the Front in order to meet the food requirements of the organisation and also as centres of agricultural experimentation to be put to the service of the peasant masses.

Urban Organisation of a new type

In 1977 the EPLF started to liberate several important Eritrean towns. As with the countryside, liberation was preceeded by a study of the socio-economic and political conditions and by a building of secret cells. Following liberation, priority was given to the mobilisation and organisation of the residents into mass organisations according to the social classes or groups to which they belonged: workers, small traders and merchants, women, youth and others. Here, we will outline the efforts by the Front to transform the socio-economic relations in the towns and to organise their political and administrative life. In this regard, Keren, the second largest Eritrean city, represented a major testing ground for the EPLF.

In the socio-economic field, the most urgent task for the Front was the city's reconstruction and an improvement in the living conditions of the inhabitants. In concrete terms, this included the maintenance of the water supply, the supplying of residents with essential commodities, and ensuring adequate supplies of fuel for transport and power installations. Despite enormous difficulties and the Ethiopian army's constant bombing of the city, the Front managed to get some factories and economic installations (the fighters joined the workers to run them), health centres and schools going. During the month following the liberation of Keren, the Front's teams worked throughout the city to repair the damage done in the fighting. Electricity was turned back on, telephone services restored, and emergency food rations were distributed. It was not long before life began to return to normal. With Eritrean families from the towns under Ethiopian occupation flowing towards Keren, the city grew rapidly. Two measures taken by the EPLF to transform Keren's socio-economic conditions are worth explaining. Firstly, the EPLF took under its direct control all the economic and financial establishments and public property that were formerly nationalised by the present Ethiopian regime. Despite all the difficulties imaginable, the EPLF proceeded with this programme of nationalisation right after the city's liberation. The ELF in the towns that it liberated instead restored all the property which the Ethiopian regime had taken under its control to the former proprietors. The second important measure taken by the EPLF in Keren was the increase of

workers' wages and the establishment of a policy of low prices for
goods in circulation in the city. On the price issue, the Front set a minimal profit rate (10%) for the city's big merchants and at the same time
created a chain of cooperative stores where food prices were about
30% less than those in private shops. The aim of this policy was not
only to ameliorate the living conditions of the city's residents but also
to combat any profiteering and speculation, and to stop opportunities
in Keren for small scale private producers to accumulate wealth.
Besides the socio-economic question, the EPLF was also confronted
with the political and administrative problems. The months following
Keren's liberation were characterised by intense political agitation.
Political rallies attended by thousands of people were held. We understand that in Keren alone fifty political and educational sessions were
held each week. The mobilisation and the organisation of the masses
was carried through on a big scale and various mass organisations were
formed. After studying alternative systems, the EPLF adopted what it
called the 'popular self-government system'. Keren was divided into six
districts each one having five mass associations: a Worker's Association,
a Peasant Assciation, a Petty Bourgeois Association, a Women's Association, and a Youth Association (16-25 years). Each of these associations
worked through a network of cells with up to sixty members in a cell.
Each group elected its leaders who together with the leaders of the
other groups elected the executive body of the mass organisation.
The members of these executive bodies joined with their counterparts
in the other four mass associations to form the people's assembly composed of thirty-six representatives. These in turn elected an executive
committee with twelve members, the high local authority in charge of
civil justice, economic affairs, security and public order.
     The EPLF felt that this system was an appropriate means of changing
the class relations in the city in favour of the revolution. By their sheer
numerical majority and the revolutionary political orientation of the
mass organisations, workers, progressive elements of the youth and of
the women were heading the political and administrative structures.
For the EPLF, the people assumed political power through their mass
associations. Although this system has been used as a model for other
towns, the Front leaders reaffirm that it does not preclude the election
of a People's Assembly in independent Eritrea by universal franchise, as
stipulated in their programme.
     It should be remembered that the armed struggle started at a time
when the working class movement was weakened and Eritrean workers
dispersed. The armed struggle was not a direct continuation of the
struggles waged by the working class movement of the forties and
fifties. Although an important majority of the working class in Eritrea
is found in the cities under enemy occupation, the control of some
towns provides the Front with the opportunity to better organise this
class. The EPLF has also done significant work mobilising and organis-

ing immigrant Eritrean workers in foreign countries. Besides their political activities, the Worker's Associations outside Eritrea play an important role in the struggle by their considerable material support to the Front. As for the workers under Ethiopian occupation, they organised in clandestine cells in factories and other enterprises. It is common knowledge, for example, that the material necessary for the running of the Front's handicraft industries and mechanised farms in the liberated areas was obtained during the frequent raids of the cities with the close collaboration of the organised workers.

The EPLF makes considerable efforts to disseminate a working class ideology. It attaches great importance to the recruitment of workers. Besides their participation in all the activities of the Front, the part played by the worker-fighters in the organisation's notable economic activities (various workshops, transportation, construction, arms and electronic repair, etc.) should be stressed. As to the leadership role of the working class, among the fighters and the members of the mass organisation that go to the cadre school, priority is given to workers or to fighters of working class origin.

D. The Liberation Struggle and Women in Eritrean Society

Many observers of the Eritrean struggle have described the participation of women in the revolution led by the EPLF as very important and quite original in the history of liberation movements in Africa. This is one of the reasons why we think the subject of women's role in this liberation struggle would be an interesting case for a detailed social and political study. For the moment, however, let us briefly see the problems posed by women's place in the Eritrean society and how these are being tackled by the EPLF.

1. Women in Eritrean society

In rural Eritrea, women are excluded from ownership of any means of production and are either excluded from social production or play a role secondary to that of men. In the highlands of Eritrea, for example, women were generally excluded from direct ownership of land in all of the three forms of land tenure. However, they spent the whole day doing heavy work on the farms alongside their husbands and/or parents. At the end of the day, the wife went home ahead of her husband and began another cycle of domestic work. In the lowlands, women were confined to the inner parts of the houses so that no man could see them. In the urban areas, there was a small percentage of women who worked in the factories. But they were usually employed as cheap labour and were thus the most exploited members of the working class.

In all aspects of political and social life, women had no place. In the highlands, for instance, women were not allowed to attend the village assembly. In such patriarchal and semi-feudal society, marriages, which are basically influenced by economic calculations, were arranged without consulting the future bride at all. In rural Eritrea, child marriages are still prevalent. As for divorce it is totally the man's prerogative.

2. Changes in the status of women

We will not deal here with the participation of Eritrean women in the liberation struggle, but briefly see how the transformation of the social structure of society that is taking place tries to bring about changes in the status of women.

We have seen that a section of the landless peasants were women. In the land reform that is being carried out, distribution of land is no longer made on a household but on an individual basis. Because of this modification in the rules of land redistribution, women have been able to receive an equal share of land. Through the implementation of land reform, the EPLF believes that one of the main causes of the oppression of women, exclusion from land ownership, will gradually be abolished. Now women are not only allowed to attend but actually do participate actively in the village assemblies and in all the social and political activities (land reform, the overthrow of feudal political power, etc.) of the village communities. In the liberated towns, women through their mass association have got access to the highest responsibilities in the organs of the self-government system. Since 95% of Eritrean women are illiterate, the efforts to combat illiteracy constitute an important factor in the emancipation of women. The marriage legislation that the EPLF promulgated in 1978 is totally contrary to the laws and traditions of the patriarchal society. According to this law, forced child marriages are, among other things, abolished in the liberated zones. As to divorce, it no longer depends only on the will and whim of the man.

The EPLF believes that these changes will be reinforced by the struggle that is waged to abolish prejudices against women in the society. These prejudices have already been shaken by the impressive participation of women in the armed struggle. Today no less than 20% of the EPLF fighters are women. Women fighters in the EPLF are also engaged in agriculture, and in handicraft industries. They work in machine shops, electrical shops, weapon's repair shops. Women fighters actively participate in military operations. In the EPLF, there is no work that is considered as being only for men. The Front also seeks to increase the number and improve the quality of women leaders. They get the first priority to go to the Front's cadre school. At the First Congress of the EPLF 11% of the delegates were women. One of the most active mass associations of the Front is in fact the Women's Association.

E. Ethnicity and Religion

Several ethnic groups coexist in the country and the various colonisations have played on the differences and even on the antagonisms between them. Different economic activities, ecological locations, cultural traditions and languages characterise the various national groups. This is a question that the EPLF could not avoid. It has taken some important measures in order to give to each group equal possibilities of expression, especially with regard to language.

The same can be said about religions. Christianity and Islam are the two main religious groups. They have both integrated elements of the traditional religions. The Coptic Church is the major christian groups, some small catholic and protestant groups also exist. In order to analyse this question, which is quite central, not only for the nationalities, but also for some aspects of the social infrastructure (notably education), an historical background would be necessary. The EPLF has not written very much about this matter, but it has a praxis which seems to be clear: respect for religious institutions that played important functions in the society. Again, this must be the object of further investigation.

CONCLUSIONS

The long struggle of the Eritreans has been largely ignored by public opinion for a considerable time. What is more, the social dimensions of that struggle are little known. More attention is given to the military aspect of it. This has created several confusions, among others the accusation that it is a purely nationalist enterprise. In this preliminary study we have tried to show this other dimension has been central to the activities of the EPLF.

Thus the decolonisation process is linking together national goals and those of social transformation. The EPLF can then be situated within the great tradition of liberation movements like the ones of China, Vietnam, Cuba, Guinea Bissau, Mozambique, and Angola. To a certain extent, it has been able to profit by their experiences. However, it also appears to have given much attention to the specificity of its own situation.

The social dimension of the Eritrean struggle means much more than a preoccupation with social problems. It is linked with changes in the mode of production. This is the reason why a class analysis is made, and why it is carried on in detail in each region before beginning the process of change. The coherence of the policies and the prudence in their implementation have impressed many observers from outside. This suggests that the Front is aware that the outer transformation of the productive relations is not enough and that there will be no solid solution without profound and patient action at the superstructural level.

This is why historical, anthropoligical and sociological research are fundamental for the long range success of the revolution, if the Front does not want to be confronted with the necessity of imposing from above solutions not yet understood nor easily accepted by the base.

The great complexity of the Eritrean social formation does not allow any bypassing of such a perspective.

We cannot forget that the task of the liberation movement has to be accomplished in very adverse conditions: war with Ethiopia, difficulties due to the divisions in the liberation struggle (not unrelated either to the class structure), intervention by the USSR in the battlefield, etc. Such internal and external conditions are making the struggle not only difficult but exceptionally heroic, the most painful contradiction being the fact that socialist countries have taken arms against Eritrea's national and social liberation.

Bibliography

G.K.N. Trevaskis, *Eritrea: A Colony in Transition*, Oxford University Press (London, New York, Toronto) 1960.

Association of Eritrean Students in North America, *In Defence of the Eritrean Revolution*, 2nd ed., New York, 1978.

EPLF "Class Analysis in the Eritrean Countryside". June 1975.

Bimbi, Guid, "I contadini di Medri Zien", *l'Unita*, Rome 2-6 March, 1977 in *Revolution in Eritrea*, Le Comité Belge de Secours à l'Erythrée, Bruxelles, 1978; "Organisation des Zones libérées de FPLE", Dossier du Colloque sur l'Erythrée, Paris, 1978.

Dan Connell, "EPLF sets example in liberated Eritrean City", "How the EPLF organizes in Eritrea", "Liberation in an Eritrean village", *The Guardian*, New York, 13 July – 16 November, 1977, in *Revolution in Eritrea, op.cit.*

Mary Dines. "Eritrea, War on Want Report", London, 1978.

P. Gammachio, "La Resistenza Eritrea", Edizioni Lerici, Cosenza, 1978.

Jean-Louis Peninou, "La Réforme agraire à Azim", *Libération*, Paris, 14-15 October, 1976; "Le test des villes", *Libération*, Paris 23-29 November, 1977 in *Revolution in Eritrea, op.cit.*

Association of Eritrean Students in North America, "Eritrean Peasants intensify class struggle", *Eritrea in Struggle*, Vol.II, No.3, December 1977. "New Keren: the fruit of a revolutionary war", *Eritrea in Struggle*, Vol.II, No.5, February 1978.

Eritreans for Liberation in North America, "Women and Revolution in Eritrea", *Liberation*, Vol.VI, No.4/5, March-June 1977. "EPLF serving the masses on the medical Front", Medical report, October 1976.

Colette Braeckman, *Le Soir*, Bruxelles, 15-23 July 1977.

André Claude, *Le Journal de Genève*, 17-19 August, 1977.

Jean Brutsaert, *La Cité*, Bruxelles, 23-26 October, 1977.

Attilio Wanderlingh, *Il Manifesto*, Roma, 7-21 September, 1977 in *Revolution in Eritrea, op.cit.*

Agriculture
in the
Eritrean Revolution
Tony Barnett

In Eritrea, where the armed struggle has gone on for so long, and where the majority of the population exists by farming, agriculture occupies a crucial position in relation to the struggle. The Eritrean revolution is seen and experienced by the EPLF as both a social and national revolution, and within this revolution, agricultural production policy aims at self-reliance and a contribution to the planned economy. Within these broad aims, three tasks can currently be identifed:

(i) the need to maintain production in order to support the population
(ii) reconstruction of infrastructure damaged or neglected in the course of the fighting
(iii) construction and transformation in order to develop the new society.

The material on which this paper is based was collected during a visit to Eritrea in December 1977 and January 1978. The time was short, and the course of the war has temporarily altered some of the specific features of the situation since then, but as the EPLF still has control of the countryside and of the majority of the Eritrean population, the general features of the agricultural situation have not undergone any radical alteration, although production has been disrupted by Ethiopian bombardment and the ebb and flow of the war.

This note outlines the types of agriculture practised in Eritrea together with the indication of some of the problems faced and some of the progress made in constructing a socialist society. The types of agricultural production system in Eritrea reflect the ecological diversity of the region as well as its colonial history. Three types of production can be distinguished. These are a highland system, a lowland system and the plantation sector. Such a distinction must be schematic, and there are of course transitional types as well.

The Agricultural Production System of the Highlands

The majority of the population in the highlands are involved in settled cultivation. However, there are in addition, some nomads, such as the Blin people, who also live on the plateau. It is important to note that some of the settled people are also transhumant for part of the year. The main crops cultivated by these farmers are wheat, barley, millet, teff, maize and potatoes. They also keep some animals and grow cash

crops such as coffee and fruit. However, the keeping of cattle and
the cultivation of cash crops is related to the class position of the
different sections of the population.

Broadly speaking, the land on the plateau has been held under two
systems. These are *risti* and *diesa.*

Risti is a form of private ownership, where land is held by a particular family, and cannot be sold or otherwise alienated except with the
consent of that family. This system of land holding is the minor one,
the dominant one being the *diesa* system. This is usually described as
a communal system of tenure. In principle, it is a system where land is
held by the village in common and is redistributed every seven years in
order to take account of changing needs of the families of the village.
In practise, this system may never have worked in this way, as the families who had charge of village affairs, represented in the village assembly
by their senior menfolk, would doubtless have ensured that the system
worked to their advantage. This is particularly the case when such a
system comes into relationship with a capitalist sector, where means of
accumulation of wealth and power are available outside of the imme-
diate local or regional economic system. And this is precisely what
happened in Eritrea during the colonial period, under the rule of the
Italians, British and Ethiopians.

In the highland villages, a four-fold differentiation of the population
developed, consisting of rich, middle, lower and landless peasants. The
rich peasants came from the founding families of the village, the
restegna, and formed the bulk if not all of the members of the village
assembly. These men would normally have owned cattle, shops, mills
and other trading assets. They were able to manipulate the *diesa* system
to their advantage, and to pass their wealth onto their sons exclusively.
If they had any *risti* land, it would have been shared between sons and
daughters. The relatively large areas of land that they controlled were
worked in part by hired labour, in part by share cropping, the labour
coming from the lower or landless stratum. In addition to considerable
control of land this group also owned implements and draught animals,
and was a major source of various forms of credit to others in the village.
In addition, the church also had areas of land which were cultivated
by hired labour or share-cropped. It is no coincidence that in some of
the highland villages, the large white building of the church looms over
the mean huts of the people, symbolising yet another form of domination and exploitation.

The middle peasants often had patronage relationships with the rich
peasants, and in many cases obtained through these relationships access
to more land than they could till with their family labour alone. They
might have had four or five oxen, 10-15 cows, sheep and goats. With
such resources they would have been able to cultivate enough land to
produce a marketable surplus. In addition, they may have hired labour
and had small holdings of cash crops.

The lower peasants would typically have had only one or two oxen and would thus have had to cooperate with others in similar circumstances in order to have sufficient draught power to cultivate their land. With few if any cattle, their land would not have received the manure available to those who had large herds of cattle. For many, their land area was insufficient for their needs, and they would have had to borrow money, or work as labourers on the farms of the wealthier people.

The landless peasants were those who were young, disinherited by the division of holdings, returned labour migrants, and above all women. In general terms it would be true to say that the land-holdings of those strata which had land were as follows. A rich peasant might have had an average of three hectares, the middle peasants about 1.5 hectares, and the poor peasants rather less than one hectare.

This system of production, and the attendant class structure, is characteristic of the settled villages, and of those communities in which transhumance is practised during their period on the plateau. However, although the main base of these transhumants is in the highlands from March to October, sections of the population move down in November until February, to the slopes at between 800 and 1000 metres to cultivate crops of maize and some millet. Here the land-holding system seems to have been rather different, based on the control of land under the *demeniale* system of government leasehold introduced by the Italian colonial administration. These holdings were in effect concessions let to those who could afford to pay the taxes and bribes involved. Clearly these would have been the rich peasants, for whom such concessions constituted another potential source of accumulation. The rich peasants would have held most of these concessions, sub-leasing some of their land to middle peasants who may have held an average of half a hectare. The actual work would have been done by the poor peasants and by the landless. The symbols of differentiation of wealth and life style will have been evident in the style of the journey from the plateau to the slopes. The poor would have walked down, perhaps with a donkey and some small stock, whereas the wealthy would have travelled with camels and their other stock.

This outline of the production system of the highlands serves as a base from which to consider the changes which the EPLF has wrought in order to push forward the idea of social and national revolution. The two examples which stand out and which have been most fully reported are the villages of Azim and Zager. A full description of the changes in Azim has been given by Jean-Louis Peninou[1] and of Zager by Dan Connell[2] and by a film crew from the British television company ATV[3]. All these reports show a process of political analysis within the villages, political education and organisation, and a movement towards control of the villages by those who form the majority of the population. Writing of Azim, Peninou described a situation where there had not been a redistribution of the land under the *diesa* system since 1922. With the disintegration of the customary system, many land disputes and cases of injustice had accumulated, until by 1975 about 850 families had some kind of title to some land, while in excess of 600 families had no land at all, and were reduced to selling their labour or migrating in order to survive.

By November 1975, the EPLF had achieved a level of organisation and education within the village sufficient to ensure that the peasants would decide to undertake a land reform. It was also decided that certain categories of people would be excluded from the new distribution, and their land would, in fact, be expropriated. These were: those who were fighting with the Ethiopians, together with their families; the 'compradors', in this case five rich men who were known as such throughout the village; those who had land in other villages. In all, according to Peninou, about three hundred heads of household were thus excluded from land holding in the village. The remaining 1,200 then proceeded to distribute the land equitably between them. The problem of church land was solved along similar lines. In a village with a total population of five thousand people, there were about fifty priests and this was an important problem. The villagers decided, in consultation with the EPLF cadres, that priests could have land on two conditions: that no priest had more land than a peasant, and that the priests were to cultivate the land themselves.

The two cases in which this type of organisation and land reform have been reported in detail are Azim and Zager, but similar attempts have been made throughout the highland region of EPLF-controlled Eritrea. In the circumstances which have followed the strategic withdrawal of EPLF forces from Keren and other major towns these two villages have been forced to become even more self-sufficient than they were before. Supplied with their meagre inputs by animal transport and at night, their isolation from the markets of Eritrea has increased.

The ATV film crew which visited Zager in September and October of 1978 reported on the beginnings of communal production with people coming together to share draught animals and implements. In some cases, it seemed, families were producing jointly on pooled land. During the early part of 1979, however, the peasants at Zager, who had traditionally worked land in the fertile Filfil river area, were forced to leave their fields and crops untended as Ethiopian bombers strafed them and set light to their crops. This situation continues to hamper production.

What is certain is that while the EPLF undertakes the initial organisation and politicisation in the villages, in particular ensuring that the representation of classes in the village assembly is in proportion to their numbers in the community as a whole, the community is quite able to take initiatives and carry on a dialogue with the EPLF cadres who are living and working in the village. This was quite apparent in the documentary about Zager which was prepared by the ATV team, and also in meetings which I attended in villages in the Eastern lowlands.

The lowland production system: flood irrigation and nomadism

On the eastern side of the Eritrean plateau the land falls away in a sudden and abrupt scarp. In a few miles, it drops about 2,000 metres, into the desert plain which extends from the base of the escarpment to the Red Sea. Such a sudden transition in altitude obviously gives rise to a similarly sudden change in agriculture. From this escarpment, a number of seasonal rivers flood down onto the plain perhaps a dozen times in a year. Unless the water is harnessed and channelled, it rushes out into the desert, and disappears into a massive soakway. The main rivers which bring water down to the area are the In, the Laba, and four smaller ones. These enable six areas at the base of the escarpment to be cultivated.

With the coming of the Italian colonial government, the whole area was declared *demeniale,* but the majority of the population were in any case 'nomads'. The beginnings of irrigated agriculture in the area are comparatively recent, around 1908 in the case of Sh'eb area, around the outflow of the River Laba, and probably not very different for the other cultivated areas of Kufrullah, Abarara, Tomboussa, Gedghed and Shebbah. In the case of Sh'eb, it appears that an Arab, a Yemeni, called Ahmed Abu Sheneb, came as a kind of technical adviser to the area and showed the people how to build embankments in the mouths of the rivers so as to split the flow, and then divert the water into shallow canals, onto extensive systems of terraces. The outcome of this is really very spectacular. Large areas of land have thus been brought under cultivation, on what is in fact rich silty soil. The areas concerned total something in excess of 10,000 hectares and in 1978 were supporting and being worked by a very depleted, but all the same extensive, population of about fifty thousand people. The area is very productive as long as there is sufficient control of the water supply, and it can produce as many as four crops in a year. The main crops are sorghum and maize followed by melons, tomatoes and other minor crops such as sesame and vegetables. If the water is abundant and the control adequate, then a final crop of water melons, as many as 25,000 to the hectare, can be produced.

The total population of the area covered by the six villages mentioned above, is in the region of 50,000 people. In the sixteen years since the Ethiopian depredations in the area began, the population has decreased by about 22,000 inhabitants, largely as a result of flight from the fighting, but also because large numbers of people have been killed by Ethiopian air raids and ground forces. As one peasant at Gedghed said:

Before the war began it was rare for a family to exeed six people.

Today the average is nearer ten people because so many children have lost parents as a result of the war. Each family used to have at least a pair of oxen to do the work. Today it is necessary for three families to share a pair of oxen.

The agricultural production cycle in the Eastern lowlands

The Eastern lowlands are seen by the EPLF as the main potential grain bowl of the whole country. For this reason they are of prime importance in overall agricultural strategy, for they hold out the hope of self reliance in basic foodstuffs. They are also of major importance in any future social reconstruction, for they are likely to be areas of resettlement for many of the refugees currently living in camps outside Eritrea.

The agricultural cycle is complex, in a way that is characteristic of irrigated agriculture. It always seems to demand at least a minimal amount of cooperation and coordination in order to maintain control of the water as well as to perform the cultivation itself. For this reason, the agricultural cycle will be described in some detail, month by month.

> **January** The first task is the ploughing in of the stubble of the previous year's millet crop. This is done prior to preparation of the land to receive the maize crop. The maize is sown, as early as possible, in order to catch the rain which falls at this time. It is followed by the sowing of groundnuts (a crop which should grow well in the area, and which could provide a source of export revenue) and some sesame, a source of oil for local consumption.

> **February** The dominant work during this period is the repair and maintenance of the main barrage and the smaller diversion structures. This is particularly important as it is possible that an early flood may occur, and unless the diversion structures are adequately maintained at this point in the year, the seeds which have been planted and which have begun to grow, could be washed away.

> Given the urgency with which the work is done, and the scale of the main earthworks, it requires large scale organisation of people and animals. The main dyke at Sh'eb, for example, is made of boulders, tree trunks and earth. It is about 400 metres long and about 15 metres high and must withstand flows of about 1.5 cubic metres of water per second maybe fifteen times a year. Such work requires between 150 and 200 people at a time, together with their oxen, working long hours in order to ensure the strength of the embankment. In addition to this demanding work, farmers are simultaneously concerned with the repair and maintenance of the small embankments in their own plots, as well as the weeding of the maize which was planted in January.

> **March** The task of maintaining the diversion works continues, as does weeding the maize and harvesting the groundnut crop, together with various legumes.

> **April** The continuous labour of maintaining and strengthening the irrigation works continues. The maize is harvested, threshed and put into storage. Ground-nuts are harvested. In the final days of the

month, if there is still sufficient water in the soil, the water melon crop is planted.

May and June As well as continuing work on the irrigation structures, a crop of sorghum for forage purposes is sown.

July The water melons are harvested. The final work is carried out on the earthworks, for by now the rains are imminent in the highlands, and the rivers will soon be in flood.

August This is the busiest month of the year. The first week is concerned with the preparation of the land in individual plots prior to the arrival of the water. It is essential at this stage to ensure that the secondary distributor channels from farm to farm, and the bunds within farms, are ready in order to facilitate the control of the water at the field level. An additional task is the repair and preparation of the wells for drinking water. At this time of year additional labour comes into the area and the demands for drinking water increase considerably. The fodder sorghum is harvested, and then the first floods are led onto the land, moistening it prior to the planting of the main millet crop for the human population. This is a time when the work is at its most unpredictable. Particularly powerful inundations may breach the earthworks, and this often requires a second or even a third sowing of millet, as well as the demanding labour of repairing breaches in the irrigation works. As the whole system depends on a gentle north-south slope of the land away from the river mouth, a breach in a dyke at a high point of the system will, unless hastily repaired, threaten to wash out the farms below the breach. In addition, while the system can channel water, it offers no escape and flooding can be frequent. At Gedghed I saw a place where this had happened, and where there were insufficient workers available to repair the breach. As a result, a deep ravine about 3.5 metres deep had appeared in the middle of the cultivated area.

September Continuation of the same kind of work as in August, in particular, the repair of the dykes and the replanting of areas which may have been washed out by the uncontrolled flood water.

October and November Several weedings of the millet crop, and continuing attention to the earthworks, although by now the flow of the rivers is beginning to abate.

December This is the month when the millet crop is harvested and processed for storage. The harvest has to take place before the millet is properly ripe. This is for two reasons: the rate of infestation by pests is very high at this time of the year; and the rains are about to commence, and the resulting dampness is likely to encourage the growth of harmful fungi in the grain. Thus it is essential that the crop is harvested while still immature, and as a result the crop is not suitable for use as seed in the next season. This means that each year fresh seed has to be purchased and brought into the area, usually from the Sudan.

The organisation of production in relation to this agricultural cycle is complex and difficult to describe for a number of reasons. First of all, the history of the area is unclear, and thus the nature of the social formation is not known in any detail. It is said that prior to the coming of the Italians and prior to the Yemeni irrigation advisors early in the century, the people of the region were 'nomads'. Whether or not this is the case, and what ther term 'nomad' meant in this particular case are both important questions. From discussions with the people in the area, it seems clear that the 'nomads' were never entirely nomadic, and certainly were not self-contained, but rather related their production to that of the settled cultivators of the highlands, through trade of various kinds.

Thus, the simple category of 'nomad' is likely to be seriously misleading insofar as it ignores the relationships between one mode of production and another. In a recent article, Asad[4] has begun the important process of questioning the use of the category, both in relation to the internal dynamic of this kind of relationship between people and nature, and also in relation to the links between such people and the wider social formation. A second, and related problem is that the area has undergone such radical changes in the last fifty years – the control of the land through the *demeniale* system, the widespread disruption and population movement associated with the war and most recently, the processes of politicisation and organisation instituted by the cadres of the EPLF.

Under the *demeniale* system, farmers took their land from the state on an annual lease. Differences in holding developed for a number of reasons, one of which was clearly the ability to bribe officials. In addition, it was necessary to make annual lease payments to the state for continued occupancy. Against this historical background, the EPLF has made the following analysis of the inequality and differentiation in the societies of the irrigated Eastern Lowlands. They identify differential landholdings: peasant families with less than one hectare of land, those with from one to 1.5 hectares, and the larger, richer peasants with more than three hectares. Today the EPLF controls the land together with the representatives of the local population.

The agricultural system of the area has been controlled by means of agricultural committees of the local population for decades, probably from the inception of the development. There are elaborate systems of fines and meetings which have as their aim the discipline required in such a system in order to ensure the maintenance of the water control structures. These committees also seem to have had responsibility for the allocation of land and for the enforcement of the rules to prevent damage from occurring to the earthworks. In the past, these committees were dominated by the wealthier farmers, some of whom as well as being employers of labour, were also merchants and traders.

However, it is clear that this farming system was in no way independent of other parts of Eritrea. On at least two counts it had to have inputs from outside the local community. In January and in the July-

September period, there are very marked peaks of labour needs. Although these are now more pronounced as a result of the decimation of the population, they have always existed, and have been solved by means of some people in the community working for cash or kind on the farms of others, or in return for the use of oxen, donkeys or implements. Of more importance though is that the community seems to have been a net employer of labour. This labour has been provided by the surrounding 'nomadic' population. People who come to work on the farms are sometimes relatives of the farmers, sometimes they are families which have long-standing associations with the farmers' families. Payments for this labour were, and are, rarely in cash, but rather seem to be in kind. The details of the payment system were very confused, but it did seem to be the case that the farmers had the most power in setting the rate at which labour was exchanged for grain, because at the times of year that the 'nomads' come to work on the farms, they are either very short of grain — the period around August, when the previous year's supply is running low — or they recognise that in January (when the millet crop has just been harvested), they are unlikely to obtain a better deal later in the year. The general point which is being made here is that there are contradictions between all farmers and their labourers, as well as between the different classes of farmer within the agricultural community.

These contradictions are in turn reflected in the inequalities and contradictions within the 'nomadic' community. There is usually very definite differentiation within such communities, in terms of ownership of animals and inherited status. If this is indeed the case with the Eritean nomads, then it is inevitably the case that these different classes will have different relationships with the settled farmers. This is borne out to some degree by the fact that when the nomadic communities come to camp near the settled communities two types of activity take place between the two groups. In addition to the exchange of grain for labour, there is also the exchange of grain for animals. It seems likely that these two sets of exchanges are not between all members of the two communities equally. In fact, the exchange of animals for grain requires that the particular nomad concerned has a surplus to exchange. With those who obtain their grain by labour, the converse is probably the case — they have nothing to exchange but their labour.

A second way in which the farming community is articulated with the wider society is through the activities of merchants. As has already been noted, the variety of millet which is cultivated is unable to mature sufficiently to provide seed for the next year. For this reason seed millet is brought in each year anew, usually from the Sudan. The supply of this seed, as well as of the credit which many farmers require in order to be able to purchase it, is provided by the local merchants, who form a network for commodity distribution stretching from the Red Sea, through centres such as Keren, Nakfa and Karora into the Sudan, to towns such as Tokar and Port Sudan.

In analysing this complex situation, the EPLF seems to have paid most attention to the structure of the farming communities, and has perhaps neglected the 'nomads', assuming that they ought to be settled when the irrigated area is expanded. Whether or not this is advisable or feasible is difficult to judge, but what seems likely is that the complex alliances between the different spheres of production and exchange require more careful analysis than is provided by the dominant analysis of peasant communities simply into rich, middle and poor peasants. While this may be sufficient for the highland communities, it does not adequately capture the facts of the eastern lowlands.

The task which the EPLF has set itself in this area is an ambitious one. It is to transform it into the grain bowl of Eritrea, and to build upon the existing communal organisation to develop far larger areas of irrigated agriculture, by strengthening and making more permanent the barrages and canals, and in addition to move toward greater cooperation and ultimately collective production. The process is evisaged as involving an elaboration and specialisation of the existing committees into sub-committees concerned with seeds, marketing and aspects of community life. This will finally result in a collective production organisation (i.e. administered by the state as part of a central plan), not a commune (where control lies more directly in the hands of the members).

In addition to changes in the relations of production it is intended that the area should undergo a process of integrated development, requiring the provision of wells for the present population as well as the great increase of refugees when they return. The provision of mills will also be necessary given the potential increase in the production of grain far beyond the needs of the local population. These plans were developed at a time prior to the Ethiopian breakout from Asmara. As with the case of the highland areas, the Ethiopian advances have no doubt made communications difficult, and has certainly put back the implementation of this important and ambitious project.

The Plantation Sector

Throughout the slopes and on the plateau near to Keren, there are a number of plantations developed by Italian and other foreign settlers. In some cases this was done by personal capital, while others involved large corporations. The larger type are exemplified by Al Abaret and Makalassi, and the smaller settler developments by Sabhour. Prior to the takeover by the army in Ethiopia, these plantations were operated by expatriate owners and managers who employed Eritreans as wage labourers. The main crops were citrus and other fruits which could be exported.

In the future, the EPLF sees these plantations as having a key role to play in the self-sufficiency strategy. At present, however, the plantations are operated by the members of the Eritrean Peoples Liberation Army (EPLA) in order to provide fruit and vegetables mainly for the Army. This ensures that members of the EPLA are involved in production and also that they put less burden on the peasants than might otherwise be the case. Not that they would be a burden on the peasantry were it not for these plantation-produced foodstuffs, for the members of the EPLA are usually involved in production in the communities in which they are based. The general impression of the plantation sector at present is that it is being looked after on a care and maintenance basis, but that a clear policy as to its future has not yet been determined. This is likely to be the case with such a sector, designed in many cases to be relatively capital intensive — pumped irrigation systems, etc. — and oriented to the export market.

Agriculture and the development of policy in Eritrea

The way in which agricultural policy is developed and implemented in Eritrea can only be understood in relation to the overall structure of the EPLF, its practice of democratic centralism and its policy of combining the national and social revolutions. Democratic centralism is understood as being a workable amalgamation of broad participation by the masses through the mass associations in policy formulation, together with strong and concentrated executive powers for implementation of both social and technical change. This principle and practice is of major importance during the period of military struggle. It is seen as the model for the future.

The formal structure of the EPLF

CONGRESS
↓
CENTRAL
COMMITTEE
↓
POLITBURO
↓
STANDING
COMMITTEE

MILITARY	POLITICAL	DEPT OF	HEALTH	SOCIAL
COMMITTEE	COMMITTEE	ECONOMICS	DEPT	WELFARE

ZONAL
ADMINISTRATION

At the apex of the EPLF organisational structure is the Congress elected from the various mass organisations. It has 315 members. This body elects the Central Committee, which consists of 37 members with full voting rights, together with six alternate members who can speak but have no vote. The Central Committee elects the Politburo which has thirteen members. This body in turn elects a small Standing Committee of four people. These four people are the Secretary General and the Assistant Secretary General of the Central Committee, the Secretary of the Military Committee and the Secretary of the Political Committee. The Standing Committee is responsible for the day-to-day operation and interpretation of the policy formulated in the deliberations of the EPLF Congress. Implementation of policy is through six main administrative divisions, these are the military committee, the political committee, the departments of economics, health, social welfare and the zonal administration. Each of these administrative sub-units has in turn a number of divisions, and the Zonal Administration coordinates the activities of the various departments in each of the administrative zones into which the country is divided.

Generally speaking overall policy is formulated by the Congress which meets every two years. Policy suggestions can be brought to Congress from the mass organisation, the EPLA or from the Central Committee. Policies are discussed in this arena and general guidelines for action are arrived at. The Central Committee then oversees the direction of policy implementation, paying particular attention to the political line which is being followed. The more detailed oversight of policy rests with the Politburo which meets every month. Problems which arise within departments or in relation to new situations are referred for advice and decision to the Standing Committee of the Politburo, which meets every day. Within the Department of Economics the heads of the various sections form an Economic Commission which is responsible for the close oversight of policy in the whole department, attempting to interpret policy within the general guidelines formulated by Congress and interpreted by the Central Committee and the Politburo.

In discussing agriculture, the most important body is the Department of Economics, and in particular its agricultural section. The diagram overleaf shows the main sections of the Department of Economics, with the agricultural section shown in some detail.

The main problems which have been faced in recent planning experience in general, and in relation to agriculture in particular, appear to have resulted from the exigencies of the military situation and the demands of the military effort. There has been the growth of a departmentalist, bureaucratic mentality, resulting in poor coordination between departments. In an attempt to deal with this problem, a Planning Commission was formed in 1977. Its head is the member of the Politburo having primary responsibility for the economy. Departments now have to have research branches which develop and appraise departmental plans. These plans are sent to the Planning Commission which then makes final decisions as to priorities between departments. The

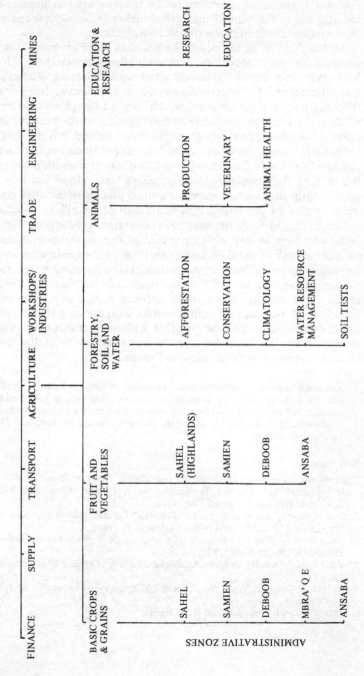

DEPARTMENT OF ECONOMICS

FINANCE · SUPPLY · TRANSPORT · AGRICULTURE · WORKSHOPS/INDUSTRIES · TRADE · ENGINEERING · MINES

BASIC CROPS & GRAINS

FRUIT AND VEGETABLES

FORESTRY, SOIL AND WATER

ANIMALS

EDUCATION & RESEARCH

SAHEL
SAMIEN
DEBOOB
MBRA'Q E
ANSABA

SAHEL (HIGHLANDS)
SAMIEN
DEBOOB
ANSABA

AFFORESTATION
CONSERVATION
CLIMATOLOGY
WATER RESOURCE MANAGEMENT
SOIL TESTS

PRODUCTION
VETERINARY
ANIMAL HEALTH

RESEARCH
EDUCATION

ADMINISTRATIVE ZONES

Planning Commission meets every six months, reviews departmental reports, and in the light of this review makes recommendations which are intended to lead to better overall coordination.

In March 1978 in the city of Keren, then in EPLF hands, the first Congress of the Association of Eritrean Peasants was held[5]. It was held under the slogan 'Consolidate the worker-peasant alliance', and was attended by 287 representatives of the peasantry, drawn mainly from the poor and middle peasants. That such a Congress could be held at all is a tribute to the degree of mobilisation of the peasants in the cause of the Eritrean Revolution. However, behind this meeting and behind the slogans there lies a solid base of politicisation, organisation and involvement of the peasantry in the affairs of their local communities and of their country. In some places land reform has now progressed through a second and even a third process of equalisation and redistribution of the land[6]. In a number of places village associations are beginning to form the basis of cooperative production. The peasants, who form at least eighty per cent of the population, now have a substantial core of militia drawn from their own communities and living and working in those communities. These members of the militia are armed, and as an EPLF cadre remarked 'the fact that they are armed is, in the last resort, their defence against any abuse by the Front'. That the peasant militia carries weapons and that the cadre could make this observation together with the agricultural and social change which has been described is some indication of the type of socialist struggle now taking place in Eritrea.

Acknowledgements The information in which this note is based was collected with the help of many Eritreans, some of whom will by now have died in the struggle. My two companions on my visit to Eritrea also contributed much in observation and discussion. They are Samuel Kassapu of Paris and Hubert Lardinois of Brussels.

References
1. Jean-Louis Peninou, La Reforme Agraire à Azien, (*Liberation*, Paris, 15 October, 1976), reprinted in *Revolution in Eritrea: Eyewitness Reports*, Le Comite Belge de Secours á l'Erythree.
2. Dan Connell, Liberation in an Eritrean Village, (*Guardian*, New York, November, 1977), reprinted in *Revolution in Eritrea* . . .
3. Documentary film on the land reform in Zager, transmitted by Associated Television, UK, 23 April, 1979.
4. Talal Asad, 'Equality in Nomadic Social Systems', *Critique of Anthropology*, 12, 1978.
5. *Eritrea in Struggle*, vol.2, No.9, June 1978, pp.1-2, *Vanguard*, vol. 3, No.1, May 1978.
6. Personal communication from Dan Connell.

The Land, the People and the Revolution

Mary Dines

It is not possible to appreciate the Eritrean situation unless one first understands its geography. Eritrea consists of a triangle of 420,000 square kilometres of land bounded on the south by Ethiopia, on the western and northern borders by Sudan and on the east by the Red Sea — the last being the clue to its international importance.

The long war has cut the Eritreans off from the outside world. The northern Sahel Province can only be reached by a two-day journey across the desert from Port Sudan. There is no road after Suakin, a small town some 60 kilometres south of Port Sudan, only a track across the desert to the town of Tokoro, nearly five hours drive from the border town of Karora. The desert track is treacherous, with sandstorms obscuring the road and large dunes building up, compelling vehicles to make wide detours. Underneath the track is, indeed, the makings of a road as far as Tokoro and periodically this appears for a mile or so, only to be lost again. The best guides are the telegraph poles that are supposed to line the road. If you keep them within eyesight, then at least you are going in the right direction. In the wet season, cars and lorries get bogged down; in the dry season, the soft sand slips under the wheels so that the tyres lose their grip and spin round and round. In hot weather, the travellers are dazed with heat. At night, in the cool season — November to the end of January — it is bitterly cold, with strong winds whipping up sheets of sand so that visibility is virtually nil.

The desert is sparsely inhabited by small groups of nomads with their camels and goats making for pastures near the river beds and water-holes. They camp out, sometimes in tents, but often in huts built with branches. At night their fires twinkle in the darkness. During the day the children are out with the herds, but the men often sit in the shelter of trees at the side of the road brewing up tea, thickly laced with sugar, which they sell to passers-by. Sometimes they also sell dates. Even at night they keep the fires going in the expectation of a lorry passing; most likely it will be one belonging to the Eritrean People's Liberation Front travelling to or from Port Sudan laden with supplies. They will always stop for a cup of hot 'shey' before roaring off again into the night. After Tokoro, the track — there is now no pretence of a road — goes off to the left through small villages and a massive sorghum project which stretches for miles. Before it is harvested it is easy to get lost among the bushes which are more like a forest than a field of crops. Between the large bushes are water-melons which only come into their own when the sorghum is harvested. Later cotton is sown on the same land. This seems the longest part of the journey to Eritrea. There are no telegraph poles for guidance, only the endless volcanic mountains stretching, greyish-brown, on the left, and clumps of thorn bush in the sand, with little settlements of nomads parking whilst there is sufficient food for their camels and goats.

The border post of Karora, which was captured by the EPLF from the Ethiopians in January, 1977, consists of a small building with a flag and two rows of barracks with trees growing both behind and in front of them. Further inside is a small forest where the animals shelter from the sun during the day. Here, the giant US-and Soviet-built trucks and lorries, captured from the Ethiopians by the EPLF, wait outside the barracks for the sun to go down, when they make a dash for the Eritrean supply lines inside Eritrea. Beyond, there is more flat desert, but this is now flanked by giant hills. These stretch endlessly into the distance. As the desert gets narrower, giant boulders appear, often huddled together in grotesque shapes. Crumbling slate has fallen away from the hillside and seems to be perched perilously on smaller rocks. They resemble many things. One looks like a gigantic lion's head with eyes and mouth; another is like an ape, and yet another like an elephant. It is hard to believe that these shapes are accidental and are not, like the pyramids or the giants on Easter Island, the work of some ancient people.

After the flat country near Korora the track rises until, hours later, it reaches the forested areas of Sahel. These areas are cut across by river beds which are full in the rainy season but almost dry in many places by the end of the year. Very little grows in the valleys except for the savannah bushes and giant trees lining the mountains. Often, these are swept away by the heavy rainfall and lie like skeletons, roots and all, on the river beds, where they are gathered up for firewood either by the Eritrean nomads wandering in the area, or by the EPLF fighters who have bases in the area. By and large, however, this area is uninhabited by civilians. Thousands of nomads were massacred by Ethiopian 'planes which flew low into the valleys and machine-gunned them and their herds to death. Today, only a few wander in the valleys, but there are many reminders of those who have died. There are myriad little cemeteries on the roadside. Each grave is a raised oblong mound of stones with a wall round it. Where there are many graves in the same spot, there is yet another wall around them all. In many areas there are also the empty shells of their shelters, built like wigwams on the sand.

Most of northern Sahel is sandy, with rivers running between mountains and vast volcanic rocks, some with bushes growing on the lower slopes, but grey and bare on the skyline. Here, Eritrean fighters guard the strategic supply routes and lie in wait for the Ethiopian 'planes which dive into the valleys spitting rockets and dropping sticks of bombs.

The river beds vary in size. Some are several hundred feet across with little islands in the middle; others are much narrower. Even in the summer trickles of water appear from time to time and patches of bright green in the sandy soil running alongside the empty river beds show that there may well be untapped wells in many areas.

In spite of the sand and rocks, there are flowers everywhere in summer — blue, white, yellow, red and multi-coloured. Many look like mountain flowers in Austria and there is a tick thistle with brilliant blue flowers. There are also many birds. These include doves, which call all day, blue and black long-billed birds that shoot in and out of bushes like swallows, red and green lovebirds and many others. Wild life is less plentiful. Wild cats inhabit the hills and come down at night looking for chickens and other food. They have giant, yellow eyes in round faces and long-striped tails. They are not frightened of man and stare disconcertingly when a torch is shone on them. The Eritrean wolf, short and grey and very fierce, is another matter. He also comes down from the hills at night hoping to steal goats from the nomads in the valleys. For this reason all nomads keep at least two dogs — yellow, short-haired creatures looking somewhat like Australian dingoes. These too are very fierce and one dog will fight off a wolf on its own. Foxes inhabit the upland areas. Further south there are tiny deer and families of monkeys. Everywhere in Eritrea, however, there are small, grey rabbits. Often at night they hop across the roads in front of lorries and the EPLF drivers slow down to let them pass. It is the camels which are a menace on the roads. At the sound of an engine they dash out of the bush and rush wildly in front of the vehicles, and they run on straight in front of them, never attempting to make for the side of the road and safety. It is not thanks to their good sense that they are never killed.

The climate in Sahel is very hot during the day, with temperatures rising into the Forties during the summer, although it is considerably cooler at night and during the winter it can be quite cold. Sahel is also mosquito country with many people there suffering two attacks a month. The sand is full of flies that bite constantly if less disastrously than the mosquitoes. The insects and heat are especially trying on the coast of Sahel, where a large Ethiopian army is still encamped after having been driven back in a series of attacks on EPLF positions in the mountains.

In the south west of Sahel lies the capital, Nakfa. This is reached over large plains from the east and west. Nakfa itself is on a plateau surrounded by mountains. It was once a town of over 6,000 inhabitants and had a piped water supply, an avenue of shops, a Mosque and a Coptic church. It is now a shell after a six-month siege by the EPLF in 1977 and constant bombing by Ethiopian 'planes which attack the EPLF fighters who are still living in the battered remains of the houses.

The hills around Nakfa are bare, with little cover except in the west where there is a forest of cacti. It is cold at night in Nakfa and in the winter a mist as thick as heavy rain descends upon the area. Further south, however, the highlands are more fertile.

Travelling south-east from the hills and plains around Nakfa you come to Alfabet. At the present time, however, the road is cut by the Ethiopian frontline about ten kilometres from Nakfa. Here some 30,000 Ethiopian troops are encamped and over the past few months they have twice attempted to break out and capture Nakfa, only to be driven back with heavy losses.

Alfabet is a typical Muslim village, with a main street of mud houses and a number of smaller streets running off on each side. Traders sell everything from single cigarettes to Omo. There was once a magnificent Swedish hospital in Alfabet but it is now in ruins as the Ethiopian army made a stand there when the town was captured by the EPLF in 1977. There was also a large school, which was renovated by the EPLF after the fighting. The town was re-occupied by the Ethiopian Army in December, 1978, when the majority of the population had fled into the surrounding hills.

From Alfabet there is a long journey south to Keren, captured from the Ethiopians in July, 1977 but re-occupied in December 1978. The journey takes about seven hours without a break and covers a great mountain range with the steepest tracks in the whole area. The EPLF encouraged the nomads to cultivate maize on the slopes. At harvest times these fields are almost red, with grey walls built up to prevent water from draining from the terraces into the valley. Every so often there are plateaux where other crops are grown. Sorghum was tried out in one place, but was not wholly successful as the water drained away. Looking over the mountain passes at night is like looking into an abyss and these plateaux bring temporary relief only to break again. Eventually, however, the road comes out in the countryside around Keren — a fertile and beautiful region, even at night. Some miles north of the city there is a large citrus plantation which once belonged to an Italian farmer, fell into disrepair under the Ethiopians and was later taken over by the EPLF, only to fall into disrepair again after the offensive in 1978. In December and January, the air is heavy with the scent of lemons, mandarins and oranges which grow in the soft sandy soil.

The way from the citrus farm to Keren runs through fields where maize is grown and where settlements of peasants live with their small herds of goats. When the EPLF were in control of Keren this was always a busy area at night. Groups of peasants would sit by fires at the roadside and come out to welcome EPLF lorries passing through with supplies for the south. 'Aouot na ha fash' (Victory to the Masses!) they would cry and often small boys in tunics would run after the lorries waving and shouting encouragement.

The road into Keren is bordered by giant round cacti with vicious prickles. Later, when streets begin to appear, the walls are lined with deep mauve or bright red azalea trees which grow all over the town. Bougainvillaea bushes also grow everywhere. Here, for the first time, are asphalted roads and stone houses. Reaching Keren is both the beginning and the end of a journey, for it was both the EPLF capital and the gateway to the South.

Keren itself is surrounded by hills on all sides. It is overshadowed by the Lalmba mountain and the giant fort built by the Italians. In many of its features it is like a town in southern Italy. The main streets are lined with large Italianate houses with gardens full of flowering shrubs. Many of these were used by the EPLF for its various administrative offices in 1977 and 1978. Then there are smaller, single storey whitewashed houses with two or three rooms, some of which are spread over the hills. There is a hospital, a beautiful ornamental garden and a large school built for orphans but damaged in the fighting and later used as a research laboratory and meeting place for the various local associations that ran the affairs of the town under the EPLF. Almost next door, however, are the conical huts of the peasants with their thatched roofs. In the centre of the town is a large market, where fruit and vegetables are on sale, and little streets of shops; many of these are run by small tailors who sit in their doorways running up shirts, dresses and other garments on aged sewing-machines for what seem to be very low prices. Other traders sell a variety of goods — some obtained from Asmara, others bought in Sudan. As in Alfabet, goods from Sudan were always transported by camel, except during the period of EPLF control when traders used to use the lorries on payment of a small fee. On the outskirts of the town is a large cattle market and abattoir. The market and the hospital, together with a school, were bombed by the Ethiopians in 1978 and many casualties were inflicted on the population.

Keren has a piped water supply and during 1977 and 1978 the EPLF got the electricity and telephone services working, but dismantled them when they withdrew from the town. There are few other services. The station is unused as the railway line to Asmara was destroyed several years ago, but the EPLF ran a bus service to towns in other areas. Damage during the fighting in 1977 was considerable, although the EPLF cleared up much of the rubble. Outside the town they even tidied up the British and Italian cemeteries, relics from the three and a half month seige by the British during the Second World War. Ironically, the British cemetery is divided into three parts — one for the British, one for the Sudanese and one for the Indians who died during the battles. The gardener looking after the cemetery ignored the apartheid and treated the whole area with the same care. After its re-occupation by the Ethiopians at the end of 1978, Keren came under the control of the Dergue who work through a vicious and repressive *kebele* system.

The road south from Keren goes through fertile country, although years of neglect have prevented it from being fully exploited. It is not until you reach the little town of Elaboret that the real potential of this central highland area can be seen. Here Italian colonists had built a large farm, growing citrus, vines and maize. There is also a large dairy. This farm was supplied with water by an ingenious water system running from a dam in the west and pipes running through the orchards and fields. The dairy farm is a splendid building with modern equipment. Nationalised by the Ethiopians, however, it fell into disuse. When it was liberated by the EPLF in the summer of 1977, fighters worked steadily to get the farm working again. The orchards were cleared of weeds and scrub, the trees pruned and a big crop of oranges and lemons was harvested and distributed to the hospitals, schools and peasants in refugee areas. Some of the vineyards were also cleared and neat rows of vines were planted. The most interesting development, however, was that of cross-breeding cattle in a large purpose-built yard with sheltered stalls near the dairy. Tens of thousands of cattle have been slaughtered by the Ethiopians, in search and destroy raids, over the last 20 years of warfare and there is an urgent need for the stock to be replenished. The EPLF were cross-breeding cattle from the Western Barka region and the highlands of central Eritrea in order to try and rear a stronger breed. They were also vaccinating cattle against TB, which they feel is essential in a country where it is estimated that one person in every family suffers from the disease.

Elaboret was the scene of fierce fighting in December, 1978. It was here that Eritrean fighters temporarily halted a massive Soviet-led mechanised drive on Keren in a two-day battle. The whole area was devastated by aerial bombardment, rocket attacks and the hand-to-hand fighting that took place.

South of Elaboret the road runs around the side of the hills, golden-orange with barley and maize at harvest-time, and with mountains stretching away to the west. After reaping the roadside is littered with piles of corn stooks stacked up by the peasants and used as fodder for animals. Camels and goats nibble at these piles, whilst others are loaded on to the backs of patient donkeys to take to nearby villages. This straw makes the road surface slippery and is an added incentive for the camels to plod on to the road and then dash off in front of vehicles. On either side of the road giant cactus trees grow, fanshaped, on the hills. As the road goes south, the remnants of villages destroyed by the Ethiopians come into sight. Some are little more than a heap of stones; others still have a few houses standing.

The Keren road goes over the highlands to Massawa branching off to the left to the capital, Asmara. Before it reaches Massawa, however, it crosses a flat plain on which lies the industrial town of Decamare. This is now in Ethiopian hands again, although the EPLF re-occupied it for a day earlier this year. Units of EPLF fighters operate freely in the countryside in this area and attempts by the Ethiopians to move troops and supplies out from Massawa are defeated by ambushes.

These ambushes cost the Ethiopians a great deal in terms of prisoners, lives and weaponry.

On the east of the main road lies the village of Woki, which can be reached up a dirt-track. This village was the scene of an appalling massacre in 1975. Men, women and children were bayonetted to death and their homes burnt; animals and crops were also destroyed. From Woki the track continues south east to Zager. This village is built on rocky highland on a ridge overlooking Asmara. The sandy soil is broken by lines of thick cacti and the prickly thornbushes common throughout Eritrea. Zager was a lively centre of EPLF activity in 1977/78 and its mass associations were a model for development.

Life in Zager starts at sunrise when goats are taken down to pastures below the village and peasants go to work in the fields. There is no water in the village so it has to be collected from wells nearby in skins which are loaded on donkeys. When the skin is full a eucalyptus branch is used as a bung and the donkeys toil up to the village where the water is emptied into buckets, empty petrol cans and any other receptacle that will hold it. The houses in Woki are mostly below ground level and consist of one room built into the hillside with a thatched roof stretched over wooden props in front to provide shelter. In this front part cooking is done over little ovens made of stones or petrol tins and goats sleep there at night. Villagers here drink coffee from the plantations to the east, which is hand-ground and then served in little pans. Some of the people keep hens, a small bantam-like variety, but most of the eggs, which are a luxury in Eritrea, are taken to be sold in the markets. Chicken is also a luxury, but, with typical Eritrean hospitality it will be cooked for a visitor.

Zager has two churches – one coptic and one Evangelical.

The inhabitants have lived through much suffering and anxiety, especially as the town is so near Asmara and subjected to air raids. They are poor, but the women are dressed in brightly coloured frocks, their hair neatly plaited across their heads and spread in a thick bun behind. They are lively and active and so stoic that they do not even look up when Ethiopian 'planes fly over.

From Woki is another road winding up and down the maintains and leading to the fertile area of Filfil. Filfil means 'river source' and describes a whole area, not just the river which rushes down the mountains, across boulders and the roots of fallen trees, later to slow down as it travels north. Here there are fruit and coffee plantations; in normal times the area is very productive. Under the trees in the valleys, the EPLF had transport and supplies for their guerrilla units and there is also a large hospital. The presence of transport makes the area vulnerable to bombing and the Ethiopians make regular sorties along the valleys. In the agricultural areas however, they make daylight rocket attacks on peasants working in the fields, sometimes using napalm and defoliants.

These southern areas of Eritrea are startlingly beautiful. Although the mountains are similar to the volcanic mountains in the north, there are many more trees, the soil is fertile and the climate less oppressive. Exquisite butterflies fly over the fields and the undulating countryside shimmers under a cloudless sky. And on the east flows the Red Sea, the clue to both the future and the tragic past of the Eritrean people.

Over 80% of Eritrea's 3,000,000 people normally live in these regions on the east side of the country, and it is here that the Eritrean People's Liberation Front has always concentrated its political and military activities. It is also in the north of Sahel that the future of the war will be decided.

In spite of its agricultural potential Eritrea is very poor. Like many Third World countries which were colonised for many years it has all the classic problems of poverty and under-development. These include disease and malnutrition, illiteracy and feudal attitudes towards women and the poor. The country's natural resources have never been fully exploited and even those that were developed — such as the fruit farms and coffee plantations — were beneficial only to a minority. The Italians exploited Eritrea's agricultural and industrial potential in the interests of Italian trade, but the British dismantled its industry at the end of the Second World War. When the Ethiopians violated the Federation in 1962 trade was organised in the interests of an élite and even Eritrean languages were forbidden in schools. Discrimination against indigenous Eritreans became widespread.

A formidable situation, therefore, confronted the Eritrean People's Liberation Front as it took over the liberated areas from January 1977. The mass of the people lived at subsistence level and wartime conditions had aggravated many social problems. The sparse medical services were largely centred on the towns and did little to cater for the needs of a predominantly rural population. Indeed, the distribution of medicine and personnel to the rural areas had fallen into abeyance in some areas. The education services were also limited and centralised; secondary education, for instance, was available only to a few privileged people.

For the Eritreans there were no instant or easy solutions. In this they were in a different position than that of many developing nations who, at independence, have international backers (usually the ex-colonial power anxious to keep the new government in power) only too ready to give aid. International relief for a country that had been at war for 15 years was no more than a trickle and could do little to meet the needs of the population. Money to build an industrial base was not available, and even basic facilities like railways, roads and dams had fallen into disrepair either through neglect or as a result of the war.

In this situation the EPLF turned to the one resource that had never been fully appreciated — the Eritrean people.

In Italian and British colonial times and during the early years of the Federation with Ethiopia, political parties had grown up in Eritrea, and although they were not able to serve the needs of the mass of the people (for the Ethiopians were already whittling away the rights of the Eritreans before the ink was dry on the international instruments establishing the Federation) they had developed a maturity that was both unusual and peculiarly Eritrean. It was logical, therefore, that the armed struggle against Ethiopian domination should have been developed by the Eritran Liberation Front as early as 1961, a year before the forcible annexation of Eritrea by Haile Selassie in 1962.

The EPLF itself was formed in 1970 after a group of radical fighters broke away from the ELF. The differences between the two movements were fundamental. The ELF believed that its main objective had to be that of winning the war against the Ethiopians and that social and political problems could be tackled afterwards. The EPLF, on the other hand, believed that the two activities had to be carried out simultaneously. In the event, the successes of the EPLF guerilla war have depended very much on the degree to which they have been able to politicise the peasants and to involve them in the social revolution that has taken place in EPLF areas. Politicisation, however, has been a slow business. For over seven years EPLF cadres from their stronghold in Sahel have lived and worked with the peasants in the countryside and with workers in the towns. The fruits of their experience and the discussions they have had were finally embodied in the National Democratic Programme. These two elements − the EPLF's National Democratic Programme and the need for flexible social organisation that could tacke under-development and cater for the needs of the population − came together in the middle 1970s with startling results.

The first problem was to provide for a mass organisation network that would be able to express the needs of, and provide a vehicle for serving, a population which had previously been divided on the basis of class, race and religion, even sex. Such divisions had been encouraged by the Ethiopians, for they could be exploited as a means of denying the very existence of an Eritrean nationality. Nor was it enough to provide a method of democratic decision-making; participation had to be built into the system. The EPLF, therefore, set up a series of mass 'associations' in the rural areas covering women, young people (youth), peasants and petit bourgeois (richer peasants and village traders, etc.) In the urban areas workers' associations were also established.

These associations deal with the affairs that affect the group concerned. For example, women's associations discuss, make decisions and take action on matters of particular concern to themselves. Each association elects its own representatives to sit on the committee running the administration of their village or town 'ward'. In this way they have responsibility on a local basis and make an overall contribution to the policy of the administration. This system has distinct social advantages. It throws up the basic needs of small communities, it provides a structure of cooperative action in all sectors and gives everyone an opportunity to express himself/herself through democratic institutions. At another level, it does much to eliminate the bureaucracy that bedevils so much of central and local government elsewhere. The degree of participation in the associations is high. This is remarkable in view of the fact that Eritrean society was until quite recently organised on a feudal basis. In particular, the role of women was an especially submissive one. Child-bearing, domestic and agricultural chores took up all their time and peasant women were largely illiterate. Few had ever travelled out of their villages. The changes that have taken place in recent years have been rapid — much faster than the gradual changes that take place when primarily rural communities migrate to towns and become absorbed into an industrialised society. These changes have, of course, been hastened by the war. The decimation of the civilian population by Ethiopian bombing and massacres, coupled with the need for personnel to man the civil administration and the fighting forces of the EPLF has meant that the participation of women is essential if manpower needs are to be met. At the same time, Eritrean women have demonstrated a high degree of political awareness and have responded militantly to the chance of liberation.

This has been a challenge for many men, who have seen their traditional role as head of the household threatened. The situation has been eased both by the support of EPLF cadres and the fact that so many women have become 'fighters' with the result that their new role as natural protectors of the community has gained wide acceptance. Arranged marriages are both banned and irrelevant, especially at a time when so many people of marriageable age are caught up in the struggle.

The democratic organisation of Eritrean society at its very base has been accompanied by the decentralisation of social services. Education and medical treatment have been taken to the rural areas, thus becoming available to all. On the education side there has been a great explosion in literacy covering the old and young alike. Adult literacy has caught the imagination and enthusiasm of the masses and even very old people who have coped with life as illiterates for up to fifty years feel the urgent need to read and write. Even those people who have been displaced from their homes (often more than once) and become refugees seem to settle down quickly to start or continue the process of learning.

Over the last few years the decentralisation of the health services has proceeded rapidly. Eritrea has all the health problems of Third World countries, but these have been compounded by years of neglect. Since they annexed Eritrea in 1962, the Ethiopians have regarded the Eritreans as poor relations and very little was done in the area of community health. A few international agencies — the main one being the Swedish International Mission — have promoted individual health projects in certain areas. One of the most outstanding of these was the hospital complex in Alfabet built by the Swedes. Nor was there any recognition of the fact that many of the health problems in Eritrea had their origin in malnutrition.

Diseases are endemic in Eritrea. The biggest scourge is probably malaria. This hits the whole population, who suffer attacks with such frequency that their general health deteriorates. Typhoid is also a severe problem and so is TB and various forms of dysentery, smallpox, measles and parasitical infections. In 1977 the medical staff of the EPLF identified bilharzia in three areas of the country, although this d sease was previously unknown owing to lack of facilities for diag- r.osis. There is also a very high incidence of anaemia, vitamin deficiency, whooping cough, conjunctivitis and haemmorrhoids. Trachoma is also a common complaint in the highlands.

At present, in the absence of facilities for vaccination, lack of fresh water supplies and malnutrition as a result of food shortages, the EPLF have little choice about how to cope with the situation. They treat diseases as they occur and make every effort to improve food supplies by the promotion of agricultural programmes all over the country. When these bear fruit they hope to see some improvement in the basic health of the people.

Great emphasis, however, is placed on health education, especially amongst the rural population. They are given instruction in methods of preventing re-infection and the spread of infectious diseases. They are also told about the importance of diet in combatting the malnutrition which makes them so vulnerable to disease. Every patient discharged from hospital receives this instruction; in the villages it is given indivi- dually to patients attending clinics and collectively to peasant, youth and women's associations by 'barefoot' doctors who make regular visits to remoter areas. The EPLF also publish a bi-monthly health manual in both Tigrinya and Arabic.

After the withdrawal from the towns, the EPLF consolidated their hospital services in northern Sahel. There are three large hospitals there. These can cater for up to 5,000 in-patients and all provide out-patient services. Mobile teams work from Sahel and still continue to provide treatment and medicine to the population in the rural areas. Every week young EPLF paramedics leave Sahel with stores of medicines and travel, often by foot or on camels, to the southern areas of Eritrea. The large hospital in the Filfil area is also serviced from Sahel.

The hospitals in Sahel are able to undertake all the treatment that is necessary to cater for the wounded and sick in Eritrea. Faced, however, with an increasing number of paraplegics and severely mutilated patients they have opened a new hospital in Port Sudan, where there are better facilities for long-term care and where nutritious food, essen- tial for their convalescence, can be more easily obtained.

In spite of the war situation, which has led to increased mobility amongst the rural population, the EPLF education services provide schooling to large numbers of children and adult literacy is still a priority.

The Eritreans speak three main languages and four minor ones, but, as already mentioned, all these were banned in school where Amharic, the language of the dominant group in Ethiopia, was the medium of instruction. The EPLF, however, believe that literacy is basic to all human activity and fulfilments. This belief is supported by the mass of the population and everyone is anxious to learn to read and write. In the villages, peasant women attend classes under the trees where they are often taught by younger people whose only aid is a blackboard and chalk. Where there are no schools the children learn by the same method in the bush. Classes are not confined to literacy, but include history and world affairs. People, who a few years ago could not even read their own alphabet, are now startlingly well-informed and ask searching and pertinent questions of a stranger.

No-one can be a fighter unless they are literate and those who volunteer (there is no recruiting by the EPLF) are educated before they undertake military training. The Eritreans have a horror of the use of illiterate persons for fighting purposes and regard the Ethiopians' 'abduction' of illiterate peasants for the Red Army as virtually criminal. Ethiopian prisoners of war are always taught to read and write by the fighters who look after them.

There is a great shortage of trained teachers in Eritrea. Many of the EPLF teachers are not professionally qualified but have learnt teaching methods from the few who are or have devised their own methods through experience. They have almost no equipment or teaching aids. In spite of this they are able to instruct children in a wide range of subjects.

The most striking example of the new educational system is the EPLF school originally at Zero. This school was founded for orphans, refugee children and children of fighters in 1976. It started with 250 children. By mid-1979, when it had been moved to a safer location in the extreme north of Sahel Province, there were over 2,500, and 500 teaching and ancillary staff.

Zero consisted of a series of classrooms built underground for safety purposes. Its walls were shored up with stone and a few steps led down to the classrooms, where the floors were of sand. Inside, there were desks and benches (many made in the workshops in the north). Each class had about fifty children. They were divided into four groups: the under fives in the kindergarten, those from 6-8, those from 9-10 and those from 11-14.

The children lived in tents or dormitories built into the mountains on the same site. They lived simply. Few had more than a change of clothes, a blanket and a mat. The walls of the dormitories were decorated with drawings, coloured cotton and a few coloured pictures. All the children, except for the kindergarten, looked after themselves, washing and mending their own clothes, undertaking communal duties such as fetching, carrying and cleaning.

The children had few possessions. Nearly all of them made little satchels of sacking, cloth or canvas. These were often embroidered with coloured wool. Some also made themselves rulers and other equipment in the school workshops. There were no toys or books, but they entertained themselves, playing games on the river bed near the school and singing and dancing to home-made guitars.

In the school areas there was a clinic and a hospital. Like their elders, the children suffer from all the diseases that are endemic in Eritrea, but malaria and typhoid are the most common. There was an isolation tent and a sick bay with about a dozen beds. All the children were given a medical examination on arrival at the school and checked daily by the medical staff. During the day they also received health education instruction.

Near the school there was an experimental garden, a miniature agricultural project similar to those being worked out all over the country. This had been created out of the sand near the river bed and the children grew tomatoes, potatoes, cabbages and carrots. Water was carried to the garden by hand three times a week and the cultivated areas were continuously being expanded.

In the classes, the children were grouped according to their stage of development and not by age. This was done because some had received no education at all before coming to the school and others had had their education disrupted by the war.

All the children at Zero learnt to read and write in their own language and in their final years were taught both Arabic and English. They also learnt history and politics, geography, mathematics, science and biology and older children had art classes.

There were forty teachers in the school, some of whom were qualified whilst the rest were trained on the spot. They worked under the most difficult circumstances and much of their work had to be done on the blackboard. There were only a handful of textbooks when the school opened, so groups of teachers prepared their own material which was then duplicated as there was no printing press. This material was adapted from a few books, often in English, on the subject concerned. Their geography texts were compiled from a mixture of English and Amharic textbooks, but put stress on learning first about their own country and Africa. They included material about climate and geology. Science books were also adapted to make them meaningful to the children whose previous experience was primarily rural and who had no access to the equipment for experiments and investigation. They dealt with elementary scientific matters, plant biology, animals and human biology.

The kindergarten at Zero was very impressive. It catered for children 3½ to 5 years of age. They came from a variety of backgrounds, but most had lost their homes and at least one of their parents. The very small children were helped to dress and wash and the staff spent a lot of time with them. When they first arrived they were often withdrawn or disturbed by the experiences they had been through and needed and received a lot of attention. Gradually they were drawn into the communal life of the school. Their clothes came from a number of different sources and some were incongruous in Eritrea. Dresses, anoraks and woollen pullovers were received from humanitarian groups in Europe and were often too large for the smaller children. Other clothes, however, were made from textiles captured in Asmara and made up in EPLF workshops.

The kindergarten dormitory was bright and large. Like so many other forms of shelter, it was built into the hills and slabs of rocks provided platforms inside. The walls were gaily decorated and there were small chairs and tables covered with coloured cloths. The children danced and learnt songs in their spare time and played out on the river bed when the air became cooler in the evenings.

The enlarged school in the north has all the main features of Zero, although it lacks purpose-built classrooms and dormitories. The children sleep under the trees or in the few tents that are available. Classes also take place in the open air. Clothes are scarcer than ever and many children wear trousers and jackets made out of wheat sacks. T-shirts and cotton shirts and dresses are patched many times and very few children have shoes. Owing to the increased number of pupils there is an even greater shortage of school equipment than at Zero. Food also presents problems as, whilst wheat and sorghum can be brought to the school from Sudan, the area is arid and it is not possible to provide the children with fresh fruit or vegetables.

In spite of all their difficulties the children flourish. There is a pronounced increase in the number of children from nomadic families and they seem to thrive both physically (being considerably taller and stronger than those living a non-nomadic life) and educationally. They now make up about one-third of the pupils.

In the West, there has been an on-going debate about the problems of minorities. There are some who believe that they will only be solved when class barriers are abolished. These people await the revolution! Others maintain that the racial situation is such that it presents a threat to society and stability and that it has to be tackled as a problem on its own. They also assume that racial prejudice leading to discrimination is a primary and not a secondary cause of instability. The Eritreans have not been able to enjoy the luxury of such a debate. As a country they have been subjected to massive repression translated into military agression on an unprecedented scale.

The nationalist war against the Ethiopians has, of course, been a unifying factor in a situation in which there are as many as nine nationalities in Eritrea. Experience, has, however, shown that in Eritrea, as elsewhere, it is not enough to be united against a common enemy. The events in the western part of the country during the Ethiopian offensive in 1978 showed that the nationalist ideal was not enough to maintain unity under attack. The collapse of the ELF and the non-intervention of Osman Sabbhe's forces were cases in point.

The EPLF, on the other hand, whilst obviously nationalistic, has, since its inception, insisted that the social transformation of society was as important to the liberation of the Eritrean people as actual physical independence. They recognised that cultural traditions are an essential part of any community and have not sought to impose conformity. Whilst acknowledging diversity, however, they have aimed at the elimination of class, sectional and sex barriers.

In the past, as I have already mentioned, education was the prerogative of the few and was only generally available to the middle classes. This perpetuated class structures, especially by the separation of 'professionals' from the semi- and unskilled. In EPLF workshops, schools, hospitals and transport depots those with skills train others regardless of their sex or origin. Tasks previously only carried out by those who have received what we might call recognised training are now also carried out by many people trained on the job. 'Squad' doctors (paramedical personnel trained in the field) and workshop technicians are a good example of this versatility, and, most significantly, skills traditionally vested in men are now also acquired by women in all areas.

Another significant factor in the elimination of class barriers has been the importance placed by the EPLF on agriculture. This was previously the province of peasants and hired hands on the larger farms where ownership was in the hands of a few wealthy landlords. Under the EPLF everyone has a period of working on the land in some way, whether growing vegetables for a small community in a fertile spot in the desert, ploughing, harvesting or looking after animals. Even the nomadic people are beginning to enter the mainstream of agricultural activity in special areas where they have been helped to terrace land and grow crops, whereas they previously subsisted entirely on money raised from rearing animals. All this has had an equalising effect on society which has proved far more fundamental than the sort of political sloganising and exhortations practised by the Dergue in Ethiopia. It has made land reform a reality in the areas where the peasants have been able to consolidate the revolution.

What are the most obvious aspects of the social revolution in Eritrea? The emergence of women as an important force in society; the enthusiasm of the mass associations; the drive for health and education; the general busy-ness of the people arising from a sense of purpose. All these are most striking. But the real beauty of the revolution shows most obviously in the warm comradeship of the people who care for each other in adversity and in their everyday lives. It is this, coupled with their heroic powers of endurance and ingenuity, that binds them together as a nation and will ensure their eventual freedom.

DOCUMENTS

The
National Democratic Programme
of the EPLF

OBJECTIVES

1. ESTABLISH A PEOPLE'S DEMOCRATIC STATE

A. Abolish the Ethiopian colonial administrative organs and all anti-national and undemocratic laws as well as nullify the military, economic and political treaties affecting Eritrea signed between colonial Ethiopia and other governments.

B. Safeguard the interests of the masses of workers, peasants and other democratic forces.

C. Set up a People's Assembly constituted of people's representatives democratically and freely elected from anti-feudal and anti-imperialist patriotic forces. The People's Assembly shall draw the constitution, promulgate laws, elect the people's administration and ratify national economic plans and new treaties.

D. Protect the people's democratic rights — freedom of speech, the press, assembly, worship and peaceful demonstration; develop anti-feudal and anti-imperialist worker, peasant, women, student and youth organisations.

E. Assure all Eritrean citizens equality before the law without distinction as to nationality, tribe, region, sex, cultural level, occupation, position, wealth, faith, etc.

F. Severely punish Eritrean lackeys of Ethiopian colonialism who have committed crimes against the nation and the people.

2. BUILD AN INDEPENDENT, SELF-RELIANT AND PLANNED NATIONAL ECONOMY

A. Agriculture

1. Confiscate all land in the hands of the aggressor Ethiopian regime, the imperialists, zionists and Eritrean lackeys and put it in the service of the Eritrean masses.

2. Make big nationalised farms and extensive farms requiring modern techniques state-farms and use their produce for the benefit of the masses.

3. Abolish feudal land relations and carry out an equitable distribution of land. Strive to introduce cooperative farms by creating conditions of cooperation and mutual assistance so as to develop a modern

and advanced system of agriculture and animal husbandry capable of
increasing the income and improving the lot of the peasantry.

4. Induce the peasants to adopt modern agricultural techniques,
introduce them to advanced agricultural implements and provide them
with advisors, experts, veterinary services, fertilizers, wells, dams,
transportation, finance, etc., in order to alleviate their problems and
improve their livelihood and working conditions.

5. Provide the nomads with veterinary services, livestock breeding
experts, agricultural advisors and financial assistance in order to enable
them to lead settled lives, adopt modern techniques of agriculture and
animal husbandry and improve their livelihood.

6. Provide for the peaceful and amicable settlement of land disputes
and inequality among individuals and villages in such a way as to
harmonize the interest of the aggrieved with that of the national economic interest.

7. Advance the economic and living conditions in, and bridge the
gap between, the cities and the countryside.

8. Make pastures and forests state property, preserve wild life and
forestry, and fight soil erosion.

9. Maintain a proper balance between agriculture and industry in
the context of the planned economy.

10. Promote an association that will organise, politicise and arm the
peasants with a clear revolutionary outlook so they can fully participate
in the anti-colonial and anti-feudal struggle, defend the gains of the
revolution, free themselves from oppression and economic exploitation,
and manage their own affairs.

B. Industry

1. Nationalise all industries in the hands of the imperialists, zionists,
Ethiopian colonialists and their Eritrean lackeys as well as resident
aliens opposed to Eritrean independence.

2. Nationalise big industries, ports, mines, public transport, communications, power plants and other basic economic resources.

3. Exploit marine resources, expand the production of salt and
other minerals, develop the fish industry, explore oil and other minerals.

4. Allow nationals who were not opposed to the independence of
Eritrea to participate in national construction by owning small factories
and workshops compatible with national development and the system
of administration.

5. Strive to develop heavy industry so as to promote light industry,
advance agriculture and combat industrial dependence.

C. Finance

1. Nationalise all insurance companies and banks, so as to centralise
banking operations, regulate economic activities and accelerate econo-

mic development.

2. Establish a government-owned central national bank and issue an independent national currency.

3. Prohibit usury in all forms and extend credit at the lowest interest in order to eliminate the attendant exploitation of the masses.

4. Design and implement an appropriate tariffs policy to secure the domestic market for the nation's agricultural, industrial and handicraft products.

5. Formulate and implement an equitable and rational taxation policy to administer and defend the country, carry out production and social functions.

D. Trade

1. Construct essential land, air and sea transportation and communications to develop the nation's trade.

2. Handle all import and export trade.

3. Nationalise the big trading companies and regulate the small ones.

4. Prohibit the export of essential commodities and limit the import of luxury goods.

5. Regulate the exchange and pricing of the various domestic products.

6. Strictly prohibit contraband trade.

7. Establish trade relations with all countries that respect Eritrean sovereignty irrespective of political systems.

E. Urban Land and Housing

1. Make urban land state property.

2. Nationalise all excess urban houses in order to abolish exploitation through rent and improve the livelihood of the masses.

3. Set, taking the standard of living into account, a rational rent price in order to improve the living conditions of the masses.

4. Compensate citizens for nationalised property in accordance with a procedure based on personal income and the condition of the national economy.

5. Build appropriate modern houses to alleviate the shortage of housing for the masses.

3. DEVELOP CULTURE, EDUCATION, TECHNOLOGY AND PUBLIC HEALTH

A. Culture

1. Obliterate the decadent culture and disgraceful social habits that Ethiopian colonialism, world imperialism and zionism have spread in order to subjugate and exploit the Eritrean people and destroy their identity.

2. In the new educational curriculum, provide for the proper disse-

mination, respect and development of the history of Eritrea and its people, the struggle against colonialism, oppression and for national independence, the experience, sacrifices and heroism as well as the national folklore, traditions and culture of the Eritrean people.

3. Destroy the bad aspects of the culture and traditions of Eritrean society and develop its good and progressive content.

4. Ensure that the Eritrean people glorify and eternally cherish the memory of heroic martyrs of the struggle for independence who, guided by revolutionary principles, gave their lives for the salvation of their people and country.

B. Education and Technology

1. Combat illiteracy to free the Eritrean people from the darkness of ignorance.

2. Provide for universal compulsory education up to the middle school.

3. Establish institutions of higher education in the various fields of science, arts, technology, agriculture, etc.

4. Grant students scholarships to pursue studies in the various fields of learning.

5. Establish schools in the various regions of Eritrea in accordance with the need.

6. Separate education from religion.

7. Make the state run all the schools and provide free education at all levels.

8. Integrate education with production and put it in the service of the masses.

9. Enable nationals, especially the students and youth, to train and develop themselves in the sciences, literature, handicrafts and technology through the formation of their own organisations.

10. Provide favourable work conditions for experts and the skilled to enable them to utilise their skills and knowledge in the service of the masses.

11. Engage in educational, cultural and technological exchange with other countries on the basis of mutual benefit and equality.

C. Public Health

1. Render medical services freely to the people.

2. Eradicate contagious diseases and promote public health by building the necessary hospitals and health centres all over Eritrea.

3. Scientifically develop traditional medicine.

4. Establish sports and athletic facilities and popularise them among the masses.

4. SAFEGUARD SOCIAL RIGHTS
A. Workers' rights

1. Politicise and organise the workers, whose participation in the struggle had been hindered by the reactionary line and leaderships, and enable them in a higher and more organised form, to play their vanguard role in the revolution.

2. Abolish the system of labour laws and sham trade unions set up by Ethiopian colonialism and its imperialist masters to exploit and oppress Eritrean workers.

3. Enforce an eight-hour working day and protect the right of workers to rest one day a week and twenty five days a year.

4. Promulgate a special labour code that properly protects the rights of workers and enables them to form unions.

5. Assure workers comfortable housing and decent living conditions.

6. Devise a social security programme to care for and assist workers, who, because of illness, disability or age, are unable to work.

7. Prohibit unjustified dismissals and undue pay-cuts.

8. Protect the right of workers to participate in the management and administration of enterprises and industries.

9. Struggle to eliminate unemployment and protect every citizen's right to work.

B. Women's Rights

1. Develop an association through which women can participate in the struggle against colonial aggression and for social transformation.

2. Outline a broad programme to free women from domestic confinement, develop their participation in social production, and raise their political, cultural and technical levels.

3. Assure women full rights of equality with men in politics, economy and social life as well as equal pay for equal work.

4. Promulgate progressive marriage and family laws.

5. Protect the right of women workers to two months' maternity leave with full pay.

6. Protect the right of mothers and children, provide delivery, nursery and kindergarten services.

7. Fight to eradicate prostitution.

8. Respect the right of women not to engage in work harmful to their health.

9. Design programs to increase the number and upgrade the quality of women leaders and public servants.

C. Families of Martyrs, disabled fighters and others needing social assistance.

1. Provide necessary care and assistance to all fighters and other

citizens who, in the course of the struggle against Ethiopian colonialism and for national salvation, have suffered disability in jails or in armed combat.

2. Provide assistance and relief to the victims of Ethiopian colonial aggression, orphans, the old and the disabled as well as those harmed by natural causes.

3. Render necessary assistance and care for the families of martyrs.

5. ENSURE THE QUALITY AND CONSOLIDATE THE UNITY OF NATIONALITIES

A. Abolish the system and laws instituted by imperialism, Ethiopian colonialism and their lackeys in order to divide, oppress and exploit the Eritrean people.

B. Rectify all errors committed by opportunists in the course of the struggle.

C. Combat national chauvinism as well as narrow nationalism.

D. Nurture and strengthen the unity and fraternity of Eritrean nationalities.

E. Accord all nationalities equal rights and responsibilities in leading them toward national progress and salvation.

F. Train cadres from all nationalities in various fields to assure common progress.

G. Safeguard the right of all nationalities to preserve and develop their spoken or written language.

H. Safeguard the right of all nationalities to preserve and develop their progressive culture and traditions.

I. Forcefully oppose those who, in the pursuit of their own interests, create cliques on the basis of nationality, tribe, region, etc., and obstruct the unity of the revolution and the people.

6. BUILD A STRONG PEOPLE'S ARMY

A. Liberate the land and the people step by step through the strategy of people's war. Build a strong land, air and naval force capable of defending the country's borders, territorial waters, air space and territorial integrity as well as the full independence, progress and dignity of its people in order to attain prosperity and reach the highest economic stage. The people's army shall be:
- politically conscious, imbued with comradely relations, steeled through revolutionary discipline,
- full of resoluteness, imbued with a spirit of self-sacrifice, participating in production, and
- equipped with modern tactics, weapons and skills.

Being the defender of the interests of the workers and peasants, it serves the entire people of Eritrea irrespective of religion, nationality or sex. The basis of this army is the revolutionary force presently fighting for national independence and liberation.

B. Establish a people's militia to safeguard the gains of the revolution and support the People's Army in the liberated and semi-liberated areas.

C. Establish a progressive and advanced military academy.

7. RESPECT FREEDOM OF RELIGION AND FAITH

A. Safeguard every citizen's freedom of religion and belief.

B. Completely separate religion from the state and politics.

C. Separate religion from education and allow no compulsory religious education.

D. Strictly oppose all the imperialist-created new counter-revolutionary faiths, such as Jehovas' Witness, PenteCostal, Bahai, etc.

E. Legally punish those who try to sow discord in the struggle and undermine the progress of the Eritrean people on the basis of religion whether in the course of the armed struggle or in a people's democratic Eritrea.

8. PROVIDE HUMANE TREATMENT TO PRISONERS OF WAR AND ENCOURAGE THE DESERTION OF ERITREAN SOLDIERS SERVING THE ENEMY

A. Oppose the efforts of Ethiopian colonialism to conscript duped soldiers to serve as tools of aggression for the oppression and slaughter of the Eritrean people.

B. Encourage Eritrean soldiers and plainclothesmen who have been duped into serving in the Ethiopian colonial army to return to the just cause and join their people in the struggle against Ethiopian aggression and welcome them to its ranks with full right of equality.

C. Provide humane treatment and care for Ethiopian war prisoners.

D. Severely punish the die-hard, criminal and atrocious henchmen and lackeys of Ethiopian colonialism.

9. PROTECT THE RIGHTS OF ERITREANS RESIDING ABROAD

A. Struggle to organise Eritreans residing abroad in the already formed mass organisations so they can participate in the patriotic anti-colonial struggle.

B. Strive to secure the rights of Eritrean refugees in the neighbouring countries, win them the assistance of international organisations, and work for the improvement of their living conditions.

C. Welcome nationals who want to return to their country and participate in their people's daily struggles and advances.

D. Encourage the return and create the means for the rehabilitation of Eritreans forced to flee their country and land by the vicious aggression and oppression of Ethiopian colonialism.

10. RESPECT THE RIGHTS OF FOREIGNERS RESIDING IN ERITREA

A. Grant full rights of residence and work to aliens who have openly or covertly supported the Eritrean people's struggle against Ethiopian colonial oppression and for national salvation·and are willing to live in harmony with the legal system to be established.

B. Mercilessly punish aliens who, as lackeys and followers of Ethiopian colonialism, imperialism and zionism, spy on or become obstacles to the Eritrean people.

11. PURSUE A FOREIGN POLICY OF PEACE AND NON-ALIGNMENT

A. Welcome the assistance of any country or organisation which recognises and supports the just struggle of the Eritrean people without interference in its internal affairs.

B. Establish diplomatic relations with all countries irrespective of political and economic system on the basis of the following five principles:
— Respect for each other's independence, territorial integrity, and national sovereignty;
— Mutual non-aggression;
— Non-interference in internal affairs;
— Equality and mutual benefit;
— Peaceful co-existence.

C. Establish good friendly relations with all neighbours.

D. Expand cultural, economic and technological ties with all countries of the world compatible with national sovereignty and independence and based on equality. Do not align with any world military bloc or allow the establishment of any foreign military bases on Eritrean soil.

E. Support all just and revolutionary movements, as our struggle is an integral part of the international revolutionary movement in general, and the struggle of the African, Asian and Latin American peoples against colonialism, imperialism, zionism and racial discrimination in particular.

VICTORY TO THE MASSES!

Adopted by the First Congress of the EPLF on January 31st, 1977